Greek cooking

ROBIN HOWE

Foreword by **Jennifer Paterson**

ANDRE DEUTSCH

First published in Great Britain in 1960 by André Deutsch Ltd

This edition first published in 1998 by André Deutsch Ltd
76 Dean Street
London W1V 5HA

www.vci.co.uk

André Deutsch is a VCI plc company
Text copyright © Robin Howe 1998
The right of Robin Howe to be identified as the
author of this work as been asserted by her in accordance
with the Copyright, Design and Patents Act 1988

1 3 5 7 9 10 8 6 4 2

Printed and bound in Great Britain by St Edmundsbury Press, Suffolk

A catalogue record for this book is available from the British Library

ISBN 0 23399 474 2

Design by Kee Scott Associates

Contents

Greek cooking

Foreword

Oh, that the food you get in the average Greek restaurant were half as good as these tantalising and delicious-sounding dishes, described in this book first published in the 1960s. *Greek Cooking* is now reprinted for our edification and, I hope, for every Greek eatery here or in Greece. Lamb is the main diet of the Greeks, and to read about succulent milk lambs, roasted delicately on spits by shepherds with their flocks, before they go into semi-fasting, makes you weep when you think of the ghastly over-cooked lumps of meat presented to you in a glutinous burnt gravy. However, following Mrs Howe's receipts will, I am sure, change all that, especially in your own home.

There are many welcome ideas for game (aside from the fact that Greeks will shoot anything that flies, including song birds and unwary chickens); hare and rabbit receipts abound, and many different ways to stuff a turkey. There is a great use of brandy in many of the dishes which is always a good idea in meaty sauces. Mezes, the national nibbles of the Greeks, are some of the best things to eat and would liven up most British drink parties. An array of tempting little dishes and gleaming olives is a welcome sight, instead of dreary old crisps and peanuts. The Greek pastries, preserves and puddings, well depicted here, are mostly dripping with honey and are exceedingly sweet and devoured by many all day long. The cheese and wines are described to help distinguish the different flavours. As we can get almost all of them here now, if you have a handy Greek delicatessen, you could try them for yourselves. The one thing hard to find in this country is a really tiny, young globe artichoke, but even this is possible.

Jennifer Paterson

Introduction

Almost everything Greek is controversial; the country, the politics, the economy, and naturally the cooking and wines.

The main controversy over Greek cooking is whether it is really Greek or of Turkish origin. For me to discuss this question is extremely difficult. I have written on both Greek and Turkish cooking. I enjoy both cuisines; I have both Greek and Turkish friends.

The Greeks base their claims to their own cooking on an older civilization. They say that when they were inventing exquisite sauces the Turks were nomads grilling bits of meat on skewers and turning milk into yoghurt in gourds slung over their saddlebags. One impassioned Greek writer explained to me, 'Lucullus came to Byzantium and brought with him the cooking of the Romans, which they had earlier learnt from the Greeks. This was blended with Byzantine cooking. Then came the Turks, who knew nothing of cooking except what they could do from the saddlebag. They sent all their cooks to Balu (a town in the Turkish interior which boasts the best cooks in the country even today) and had them taught Greek dishes. They then returned to Constantinople, called this Turkish cooking and the myth has been played ever since.'

Ancient Greece was interested in food, very much so, and in their earliest writings there is frequent mention of food and cooking. There were many famous men who boasted of their culinary ability in those days. Thimbron of Athens was one; Soteriades was another, he was something of a faddist for he liked to cook different foods for different moods. There was the philosopher Archestratus, whose *Gastrology* was a culinary masterpiece. He wrote 'for immortal Greece' and stated his precepts with the zeal of a sublime legislator. He travelled widely in his search for new recipes and new luxuries to delight his table. One of the sadnesses of his life was that he could not eat the things he liked all the year round, but he brightened up with the thought that even so, there was nothing to prevent him talking of all dishes all the year round. Many of his recipes, which must surely be of the oldest in the world, he was writing around 350 BC, are said to be in use in Greece today.

The whole of the Western world owes much to Greek cooking. We owe to them aristology or the art of dining. To the Greeks belongs the honour of producing the sages of the kitchen: Orion who invented white sauce; Lampriadas who discovered brown sauce; Nereuse of Corinth who turned

1

Greek cooking

the conger eel into a dish 'fit for the gods'; Agres of Rhodes who first thought of filleting fish; Atlantus who invented the perfect restorative, and finally there was Euthymus who is said to have created the most exquisite vegetable dishes. There were others, Artemidorus who commented on and made a collection of all the words used in the kitchens of his time. Timachidas, another Rhodean, was a cook and poet of high renown who composed an epic poem on his art. Dionysius wrote of cooking and what constituted the perfect cook in no uncertain terms:

To roast some beef, to carve a joint with neatness,
To boil up sauces, and to blow the fire
Is anybody's task; he who does this
Is but a seasoner and broth-maker.
A cook is quite another thing. His mind
Must comprehend all facts and circumstances;
Where is the place, and what the time of supper;
Who are the guests, and who the entertainer;
What fish he ought to buy, and where to buy it.

And so on.
And roughly a century later Atheneus, writing his *Banquet of the Learned*, had a great deal to say on gastronomy, quoting such dicta as:

Know then the cook, a dinner that's bespoke
Aspiring to prepare, with prescient zeal,
Should know the tastes and humours of the guests

And:

All books of cookery, all helps of art,
All critic learning, all commenting notes
Are vain, if void of genius, thou wouldst cook.

He also quotes Ana, the philosopher, who said, 'The master cook makes the nostril feel each scent distinct.'
Finally the chef's cap is said to be of Greek origin, being a white version of the Greek monk's hat. During days of persecution many famous cooks (who were also philosophers) sought refuge in the monasteries. These had a

tradition of good food and wines. The cooks in their sanctuary carried on their proud art but felt that they were men above the ordinary monk, men apart, and asked permission to wear a white cap instead of the conventional black. They were given this distinction and, as all the world recognises, the chef is known by his tall white cap.

The Greek Empire was finally eclipsed by the Roman, but even then the Greeks had their triumphs, for they took their culture and their culinary arts to Rome. One reads of peacock from Samos, crabs from Chios, Iberian chestnuts, cranes from Melos and Phrygian turkey. And yet, although the Romans inherited all the luxury of Greece, they never erected, as the Greeks did, a temple to Addephagia, the Goddess of Good Cheer.

This is the Greek case, and only part of it.

Today there is a great similarity between the food of the Greeks and the Turks, it is hard to distinguish it. The Greeks are, perhaps, tending to look more to the West these days and they use wine in their dishes, which the Turks as Moslems should not do. The grilled dishes are probably of Turkish origin, but what has actually happened is that the peoples of this region have become so intermingled as the results of succeeding conquests over the centuries that it is difficult to sort out the various national dishes. Oddly enough most Greeks are willing to concede that the Greek sweets are really Turkish, but since honey was such an important ingredient in Greek cooking, and one must not forget that it was the Greeks again who invented pastry (although the French perfected this art), I am inclined to think that they are of Greek origin.

But this is enough. Counsel, I feel, should rest at this stage of the argument.

I would not be honest if I did not admit that there are two distinct schools of thought regarding Greek food. For and against. There are no half measures. I belong, quite naturally, to the 'for' school of thought, but do realize that the 'againsts' have their points.

Greek food is apt to be served lukewarm and with too much oil for our taste. Many non-Greeks do not like olive oil but as it is an essential part of all Mediterranean cooking, there it is. I have lived long enough in olive oil producing countries to like it very much. But I do not like all my food smothered in oil. Some Greeks do. As far as this book is concerned I have given Greek quantities and you can use as much or as little as you like.

Greek cooking is seasonal with cooks relying mainly on the fruit, vegetables, meat and fish of the season.

Greek cooking

Greek meals are not as ours. They are less formal. Breakfast consists of a coffee, often black. Lunch is fairly late and is invariably followed by a siesta, then back to work until seven or eight o'clock. Dinner is always late. Most Greek men appear to eat out at least three times a week, women less often, although they spend quite a lot of time in the patisseries, which evens things out.

But Greeks do also appear to be eating all through the day. They start on their way to the office when they stop for a fresh roll from the street corner bakery stand; then they send out for a slice of cheese pie, or nibble away at nuts and small eats. And although I know that Greeks do work, most of my Greek friends work very hard, I always wonder, when in Greece, where all the people come from who are sitting around the coffee houses sipping coffee and denouncing the world.

Food shopping in Athens is fun and can be accomplished at any time of the day or night, up to very late in the evening. You can even buy flowers and have them sent to a friend well after dark. Maybe this is bad for shop assistants but it is awfully nice for the customers.

Much of the shopping for the house is done at the door. Earliest to arrive is the baker's boy who comes with the fresh sesame rolls calling 'freska koulouria' loudly as he rushes up the stairs or through the garden gate. And the house after his visit is filled with the sweet smell of hot bread. From then on the day is one long sales campaign. The fishmonger, the baker's boy, this time with the brown bread slung haphazardly over the handlebars of his bicycle, the greengrocer, the butcher, all there on the doorstep, their goods carried either by donkey or donkey cart. The fish comes alive, the fishmonger yelling with vigour, 'Ap ti thalassa zondana', which means roughly, 'All alive-o, straight from the sea', since no Greek in his senses would buy a dead fish.

There are several markets. One of my favourites is in the centre of Athens where the stalls are piled high with the produce of the countryside brought from just outside the town. Tomatoes, 'as sweet as honey', ladies' fingers, aubergines, large and purple and highly polished, are displayed side by side with white cauliflowers. Small marrows, onions and sweet peppers in all their brilliant colours; black and red cherries, lemons, melons and grapes, grapes and more grapes. Further along there is the meat market with huge dripping carcasses of sheep and lamb, goat and kid, all very young. Greeks prefer always to see what they are buying and, where there is a cold storage, the notice telling the customers what they have in stock is very large. There are game birds in plenty, and round the corner is the fish market. In front of the entrance sit little old women selling lemons, for everyone knows that if you buy fish you must buy lemons. And naturally there are huge vats of black and green olives in brine, every type of dried bean, rice and other dry goods. And always a small boy in attendance to carry your goods home.

Spices and herbs are both important to Greek cooking. Dill has been used for centuries, and it is recorded that the ancient Greeks would chew dill seeds during the interminable speeches of senators, or throughout long plays to keep themselves awake. These same ancient Greeks felt that herbs improved one's brain power and, therefore, put them in almost all their dishes. Hippocrates, 'Father of Medicine', used over four hundred different herbs in his cures and, of these, two hundred are still in use today. Tansy was one, the name comes from the Greek word *athansy* which means immortality; while thyme is the symbol of courage. It was thought that chervil, a herb with something of the flavour of caraway, was the cure for hiccups, and parsley was supposed to absorb the fumes of wine and delay intoxication. For this reason the Greeks used to garland their foreheads with wreaths of fresh parsley before embarking on a long drinking bout. Another aid against intoxication was to make wine punches in a bowl made from amethyst, why, I do not know, but the Greek word for intoxication is *methi*.

Much of the best Greek food today is found in the *tavernas* and much of the pleasure of Greek cooking is in the atmosphere. The recipes chosen for this book are the most typical. They represent everyday cooking, of the type anyone can cook. Although at first sight you might think there is not much imagination in Greek cooking, after a while you begin to realize that the Greeks have come to terms with their essential materials and made a fine adjustment with what they have.

Greek cooking

Getting Recipes
Acknowledgements

I have collected recipes everywhere, even in aeroplanes. But mainly I prefer to take them from housewives or cooks, in homes and in restaurants.

Some of my recipes have come from tavernas. Usually I would eat a dish, like it and then demand its recipe. This involved a miracle of concentration. I remember in one popular taverna it seemed as though all the kitchen staff and waiters were bent on making sure nothing was left out. Hands were waved in all directions and other diners must have wondered what on earth had happened.

'Butter fresh', the cook exclaimed. 'Not oil or any other fat', took up a passing waiter. They were describing the making of pastry. 'But, of course, only the best oil from Greece for frying or roasting', insisted another. At the mention of garlic, black eyebrows rose. Of course, plenty of this. Even with beef.

Careful attention was paid to the meat. I needed no translator to tell me what was happening as hands waved and pulled out imaginary sinews and nerves, cutting off odd bits of fat or lesser ends. 'Shrinkage results if all this is left in', it was explained.

And wine, 'Very important'. The whole staff forgot their work.

They almost shouted recipes at me, in that way all nationals do when confronted with a foreigner whose knowledge of their language is weak. Other diners in the restaurant were sympathetic; no one rapped impatiently on their table when their waiter stopped at my table to cry, 'and a very slow oven', before delivering his food.

Books on cooking are never written without a host of willing and interested helpers. I have been singularly fortunate in preparing this one.

I am not a solitary eater, or drinker, and my husband is probably my most willing assistant in any research into food, and, of course, drink. He is prepared to sacrifice himself, he says, to prove to any hard-drinking Greek villager that he can drink for three, and still walk home. He will eat for three as well. So taverna owners look upon us with affection.

Then there are always those people who have lived in countries which we visit and who are willing to give of their longer experience. Such people as John Hare, chief of the British Information Services in Athens, who speaks

Greek, knows his Greeks and the country, and where to eat. He almost shut up shop to help me, and got his staff interested too.

There was Harold Byatt, the Press officer, who spent evening after evening taking me to tavernas, explaining the ins and outs of them all. And, since he speaks Greek as a Greek, he was able to tell me what was happening all around me, making rapid translations of the many conversations we could listen in to.

Also in the same office is Mrs M. Brooks-Tsatsopoulou who translated and typed recipes from her mother-in-law's favourite cook book and gave me her own housekeeping experiences. There was Miss C. Politis who also gave me recipes, which were, she declared, special to her family.

Then there were those, like Shan Sedgewick, who took me to such spots as 'a place near Athens', and Robert Liddell, who gave me lots of general advice, although, Hellenophil that he is, he is not a lover of the Greek way of eating.

There were so many. Behind it all there was my own experience with two Greek cooks, Ketty and Valentini, both now dead but both superb cooks.

Finally there was Penelope Papadakis who so patiently and with such interest went through the manuscript correcting errors and making valuable suggestions. And Rosemary White who gave a final reading to the manuscript. Both did this in New Delhi while waiting for their daughters to be born.

New Delhi, November 1958

Greek cooking

Notes

These few notes will help in producing authentic Greek dishes.

Greek cooking is not difficult, neither is it expensive. An added advantage is that much of it is cooked and served in the same casserole. For me, Greek cooking also has the advantage that there is much elasticity in the time allowed for cooking most of the dishes. For this reason I have so often written 'about one hour'. It is difficult to be absolutely accurate when there are so many different kinds of cooking stoves.

Olive oil varies and all countries producing it insist theirs is the best. It is a matter of local taste. If the olives are of good quality, and Greek olives are considered to be among the world's best, and if they are carefully harvested, collected, stored and properly refined, then the olive oil will be good. However, those who find olive oil too heavy or of too pronounced a flavour, should try peanut oil, much favoured by the Chinese, which has little or no flavour. But, and this is a large but, when cooking dishes which are to be eaten cold and require oil, olive oil is the best, since it does not congeal.

Without the lemon, Greek cooking would undoubtedly collapse, for it is a basic ingredient and is used from the soup to the pudding. Vegetables are soaked or sprinkled with lemon juice, fish is rubbed with it to remove the fishy flavour, meat receives the lemon treatment to bring out its flavour, and lemon is added to sugar-syrup to prevent crystallization. So when cooking Greek dishes, a fair supply of lemons is absolutely essential. Lemon juice should be strained before using.

Like other Mediterranean people, the Greeks adore tomatoes for which they have some basic rules. A small piece of cinnamon is often added to a dish which has plenty of tomatoes. Equally, when tomatoes are used the lemon is ousted. Spinach and tomatoes are not used together. Tomatoes should be peeled for all dishes except for stuffing. It is quite simple to take off the skin. Simply steep the tomatoes in boiling water for about 1 minute, then take them out and peel them as soon as they can be handled.

Onions and garlic find favour in the Greek kitchen, the first are said to 'cut' the olive oil. When spring onions are called for in a recipe, use as much as possible of the green stalks. This rule also applies to celery, the leaves have an excellent flavour.

Appetizers

Chestnuts are extremely popular with the Greeks in the islands and some of the mainland districts; they are interchangeable with potatoes.

If you see 'tis-Oras' on a menu it means à la minute or 'on-the-spot' cooking.

The vinegar used in the recipes in this book is always white wine vinegar unless otherwise stated.

Mezethakia or Orektika

The word mezethakia is applied to food which is suitable for eating with wine or spirits, and which 'opens the appetite'. While this is more or less equivalent to hors d'oeuvre it is so with a well-seasoned and varied difference. Mezethakia, or mezes, are eaten at leisure to the accompaniment of ouzo or other drinks before a meal, or with wine during a wine drinking session. In a restaurant you expect, and get, a continual replenishment to the many rapidly diminishing plates or saucers of food. No Greek would think of drinking without eating.

There are some standard mezethakia such as olives, nuts and feta cheese, otherwise what you eat depends on the season, the place, the time and the imagination of the cook. Along the seashore, where tables are placed on the sand and the waves gently lap at one's feet, every conceivable variety of fish is served. Sometimes the fish comes out of a large refrigerator belonging to the taverna across the road, whose proprietor charges for his fish not by the portion but by the weight. A long session means endless scraps of paper with your final bill. As you nibble at a dish of fried smelts, or pick the bones of some grilled mullet, fish hawkers will come up to your table and offer freshly gathered sea urchins, clams or cockles. There will always be brown, coarse bread, soft and crumbly bread called karveli, very delicious and with the real flavour of bread.

Eating mezethakia often consumes an hour or two before dinner, for Greeks eat late, very late, as eating to them is a social occasion. Not for them a quick dinner before the theatre; no, the theatre first, then a long meal in a favourite taverna together with a discussion on the play, politics and the affairs of the day. Greeks are never at a loss for conversation. Eating around midnight on a hot summer night is no exception in Athens, so mezethakia helps to keep the hunger pangs at bay as well as to provide practical blotting paper for the drinkers.

Greek cooking

Olives

The fruit of the venerable olive tree has always been regarded by the Greeks as the most valuable and most nourishing of all foods. Without the olive there would be no Greek cooking. If a Greek is hungry and the cupboard is bare just give him a chunk of coarse, brown bread and a dish of olives and he will thank you and be happy.

The history of the olive is older than the history of Athens and as old as the mythological history of Greece. The Greek Goddess, Athene, after whom the city of Athens is named, owned the olive tree and when she and Poseidon fought for supremacy over the people of Athens, the gods decided in favour of Athene because she caused the olive tree to be born and was, therefore, more important to mankind than poor Poseidon who had opened up a salt spring with his trident in the rock on which is the Acropolis. In gratitude Athene was elected the Goddess of the City of Athens.

The olive symbolizes peace and with the leafy branches of the olive victory is crowned. From the olive wood the arrows of Herakles were made, the sceptres of kings and the crooks of shepherds.

However, despite this charming story I sometimes wonder who first decided that olives would make good food, for the olive when it comes from the tree is bitter and horrible. And yet, from time immemorial, olives have been put into brine and today the typical Greek olive is always in a tub of brine. And there are so many olives and so many trees. Sometimes, driving through the Greek countryside, it seems to be one vast olive grove; mile upon mile of muted olive green; mile upon mile of distorted trunks and branches which look like strange figures from another world; almost a world of Walt Disney. Travel through the areas where the olive trees grow in the early evening or through the mists of the early morning, and you will see what I mean. Some of these trees are so old, I feel they were part of Athene's first planting.

But if the countryside seems to be devoted to the olive, so do the streets, for at times they are lined with barrels of olives in brine, of all sizes and both black and green. Some of the Greek olives are as large as walnuts, and the monks, I am told, stuff them with caviare. Lucky monks. And the best olives are those which fall to the ground of their own ripeness, say the Greek connoisseurs.

One of the most enjoyable times in the country is the olive harvest which ends in singing and dancing, feasting and merrymaking. And if the harvest is especially good, spirits rise high, for much of Greece's economy depends on the olive.

Appetizers

Nuts

Among these you will find blanched almonds, walnuts, pistachio nuts, peanuts and pine nuts. Sometimes some honey is poured into a saucer and then heavily garnished with blanched almonds or walnuts, this is considered an excellent accompaniment to wine.

Almonds, incidentally, grow plentifully in Greece and are used in many ways. They are a symbol of happiness and at weddings sugar-coated almonds are offered on silver trays to the guests. Unmarried girls always scramble for them, as we do for the wedding bouquet, and when they are placed under the pillow at night the sleeper must dream of the man she will marry.

Seeds

Usually bought from the *passa tempo* man, and include dried water melon and sunflower seeds. The *passa tempo* man is the nut vendor who rumbles along with a Heath Robinson contraption which looks like a baby carriage. It is fitted with a tray, divided into sections and covered with glass. Inside the sections are the *passa tempo*, or roasted nuts and seeds, which one eats to pass away the time. At one end of the 'carriage' is a charcoal fire with a chimney, the kind of chimney that would delight Emmett.

Chickpeas

These and other smaller peas are roasted and salted.

Fruit

It is not unusual to be served an orange or an apple, usually small, or even dried and peppered figs which are brought in from Corfu. The ripe figs are dried until dark brown, then peppered and encased in bayleaves. Extremely good. From the small island of Poros, not far from Piraeus, come pickled lemons, green and bittersweet. And, of course, bowls of grapes.

Greek cooking

Fish

A good variety is available at most times of the year. Octopus, dried and grilled or cooked in a wine sauce, will be served. Also grilled mullet, mussels plain or stuffed, clams, cockles, sea urchins and smoked fish, rather salty but excellent for nibbling. There is *lakertha*, usually made either from swordfish or palamid, which is a type of pickled fish, or, perhaps better explained, a little like smoked salmon. There are delicious lobster balls, simply pounded lobster meat blended with egg yolk and rolled in ground ginger and fried until brown. Crabs, prawns and shrimps are often served with a mayonnaise sauce. Anchovies reach the table either in long strips or sometimes beaten to a purée. As well come fresh sardines and smelts fried crisply like a biscuit and, of course, taramasalata, or fish roe salad, as well as dried red caviare, cut into thin slices. Recipes for these, and further descriptions, will be found in the fish section. Taramasalata is in the salad section. Snails are not popular but from time to time one comes across them prepared as *mezethakia*. Prickly sea urchins, whose succulent orange-coloured mouthful seems hardly worth the trouble of picking out, prove worth the bother. Squids and cuttle fish covered in their inky brine are quite delicious when properly cooked.

Meat

Meat is usually served in the form of kebabs or rissoles. As well come bits of liver, even chicken livers, grilled or fried. Often there will be chunks of grilled lamb, or cold cuts of meat in aspic or brawn.

Salads

These are rather different from our own salads, and recipes for them are in the appropriate section. For *mezethakia*, aubergine purée is almost always served, so is white bean purée (both called salads), sliced tomato salad and *taramo* salad. Beetroot salad with *skorthalia* is another popular dish. Slices of potato with olive oil constitute a Greek salad, so do whole beans in oil and chopped green peppers, all of which appear in due season on the *mezethakia* list. And I must not forget white cabbage salad, well mixed with olive oil, and pickled cucumbers. Last but not least there is yoghurt and cucumber salad, called *tzatziki* (see salads).

Cheese

All varieties of Greek cheeses are served as *mezethakia* and particularly good are fried squares of feta cheese, called *saganaki*. A friend of mine thought he was eating turbot. See cheese section.

Bourekia

These are filo pastry snacks filled with various mixtures such as cottage cheese, spinach and minced meat. *Bourekia* are sometimes cigarette-shaped, or like tiny envelopes, and almost invariably fried. Extremely good.

Dolmathes

These are stuffed vegetables and are served both hot and cold and more particularly in their season. Vine leaf *dolmathes* are immensely popular. Depending on how long you are going to drink you will also get (if the drinking is substantial) pepper and aubergine *dolmathes*, although these usually constitute part of the main meal, which, in a taverna, is bitty in any case and usually shared by all around the table. However, this pleasant custom of sharing makes for variety and obviates the feeling one so often has that whatever favourite dish one has chosen, the other man's choice always looks much tastier when it arrives. See vegetable section.

Pastourmá

I have eaten this from time to time in Greece but not as often as in Turkey. It is a black, smoked bacon, highly flavoured with garlic and considered by Greek gourmets the bacon of the connoisseur. Generally it is fried until very crisp and sometimes served with eggs.

continued

Greek cooking

Sausages

There is a fairly good array of these, especially of the garlic flavoured variety, including *kokoretsi*. They are eaten hot or cold according to their type.

Vegetables

Radishes, both red and white, are served, also raw and tender turnips. The latter are served whole but thinly peeled.

A rather special kind of *mezethakia* is *peinirli* but a couple of these would certainly constitute a meal. They are pieces of yeast dough, usually pulled into boat shapes and baked, then packed with a variety of fillings. Some have eggs and ham, others thick chunks of feta cheese, or simply fried eggs, slices of sausage, etc. *Peinirlis* are a speciality of one or two tavernas on the way to Phaleron and it is worth asking one's Greek friends to give exact details.

Others of the larger snacks or appetizers are Cretan cheese cakes, made of pastry with a filling of fresh cottage cheese mixed with beaten eggs and honey, like *melopita* (see page 196). Awfully good when hot and well made and can be bought throughout the country at road stops and railway stations.

Soups
Soupa

Greek cooking

Fish Soup With Egg and Lemon Sauce

Psarosoupa Me Avgolemono

900g (2lb) white fish fillets
2 large onions
3.4 litres (6 pints) water
125ml (4fl oz) olive oil
4 stalks celery with leaves

3 carrots
Salt and pepper
Egg and Lemon Sauce
  (see page 165)
Juice 1/2 lemon

Clean and then cut the fish into pieces, not too small, and each piece more or less the same size. Rub with salt and lemon. Clean the vegetables and cut these into rather chunky pieces but even so not too large. Put the water into a pan and bring it smartly to the boil, then add the oil, stir this well and, when it is blended, add the vegetables; reduce the heat and cook steadily for 40 minutes. Reduce the heat to simmering, add the pieces of fish and cook carefully for 20 minutes. The fish should not break, so cooking must be really slow.

When the fish is tender, take it from the pan, put it aside but keep it hot. Strain the stock and vegetables through a sieve and return to the pan. Reheat the strained fish stock, add the Egg and Lemon Sauce, stir it well into the soup (not allowing this to boil) and then pour the soup over the fish. Whether you do this in a soup tureen or directly into soup plates, depends entirely on the cook.

Some Greek cooks add rice to this type of soup which makes, of course, a more substantial dish. To the above quantity of soup add 75g (3oz) of long-grain rice, after the fish has been removed and the soup strained. Cook it only just long enough to make the rice tender, then add the sauce and continue as above.

Fish Soup

Psarosoupa

A very typical Greek fish soup which provides two courses for the same meal, fish soup followed by fish.

1.4kg (3lb) white fish fillets	*3–4 carrots*
2.3 litres (4 pints) water	*4 onions*
12 potatoes	*Salt and pepper*
Handful finely chopped fresh parsley	*90ml (3fl oz) olive oil*
2–3 chopped stalks celery	

Wash and peel the onions and score them but leave them whole. Coarsely chop the carrots, leave the potatoes whole, unless they are very large, when you can cut them into halves. Put these into a large saucepan with the water, olive oil, salt and pepper. Cook until the vegetables are tender, add the fish and cook gently for about 10 or 15 minutes, according to the size of the fish. When the fish is tender, take from the pan, arrange on a hot platter, surround with the vegetables and put into a warm oven to keep hot. Strain the stock and serve this as a clear soup; or bring the stock once more to the boil and add 2 or 3 tablespoons of long-grain rice. Also Egg and Lemon Sauce (see page 165) may be added.

Greek cooking

Soup Made From Small Fish

Soupa Hanoi Avgolemono

Hanoi are small pink fish extremely popular with Greeks and considered a clean fish as they live near the shore among the rocks, unlike the red mullet which likes the offshore mud.

1.4kg (3lb) sprats
2.3 litres (4 pints) water
Handful chopped fresh parsley
1–2 stalks chopped celery
3 chopped carrots
125ml (4fl oz) olive oil

4 finely chopped onions
Egg and Lemon Sauce
  (see page 165)
Lemon juice
Salt and pepper

Remove the heads and tails of the hanoi, clean and rub each fish with salt and lemon juice. Heat the oil, fry the onions and the parsley, add salt, pepper, the vegetables and water (plus, if you like, the fish heads to help the flavour) and cook over a medium heat for 30 minutes. Rub the stock through a sieve, return it to the pan, add the fish and cook these until tender, about 10 minutes. Take the fish from the pan with a perforated spoon, put into a soup tureen or directly onto plates, but keep hot. Strain the stock, bring it to the boil, stir in the Egg and Lemon Sauce, leave for a minute or so, then pour it over the fish. Serve at once.

    This recipe appears at first glance to be more troublesome than it really is. It is the second straining which gives a false impression. Adding some dry white wine to the stock adds much to the flavour but it is by no means essential.

Greek Bouillabaisse

Kaccavia

According to the Greeks, they are the originators of bouillabaisse, which, they say, is a relic of an ancient fish soup called *kaccavia* or *kakavia* and was introduced by the Greeks to the *Marseilla Phocaem* Colonies. The name is derived in Greek from the type of earthenware pot, *kaccavia*, in which the fishermen used to cook their fish and which was placed in the middle of their fishing boats, around which they would sit and help themselves. The name was translated into the French bouillabaisse from *bouillote*, or pot.

There are several ways to make this soup or stew, some simple and others elegant. Here is one of the elegant methods.

1.4kg (3lb) mixed fish	2.3 litres (4 pints) water
2 each sliced onions, potatoes and carrots	1 bay leaf
1 chopped celery stalk	125ml (4fl oz) olive oil
1–2 cloves chopped garlic	Peppercorns and salt
4 chopped tomatoes	Juice 1 small lemon
150ml (¹/4 pint) dry white wine	3 tablespoons chopped fresh parsley
	Croutons

Clean and trim the fish and rub it well with salt and lemon. (You can make fish stock with the trimmings and use this instead of water.) Heat the oil in a large saucepan and simmer the celery, potatoes, onions, carrots and garlic for about 5 minutes. Add water (or stock), bay leaf, peppercorns (about 3), tomatoes and wine and continue cooking for 30 minutes. Strain this mixture and return the liquid to the pan, adding a little more hot water if required. Add salt, parsley and fish, the larger, firmer fish first, and cook this for 5 minutes before adding the smaller fish which may be left whole. Bring once to the boil, then continue cooking until all the fish is tender. Put a tablespoon of croutons into each soup plate, add the fish and soup, or serve the fish and soup separately, the croutons, of course, with the soup.

Serves 4–5.

continued

Greek cooking

A more simple *kaccavia* is prepared by the fishermen in the islands as they haul in their fish along the shore. First they put the small fish into the pot with water to cover, then add olive oil, chopped onions, tomatoes, if available, salt and pepper. When everything is quite soft it is rubbed through a sieve and returned as a thick stock to the pan. Into this they put all kinds of fish, including small lobsters, shrimps, in fact any fish available, then plenty of water and cook over a wood fire until all the fish is tender.

Not all of these fishermen cooks rub the fish through a sieve, some simply put plenty of chopped onions, tomatoes, seasoning, olive oil and water into a pot and bring it quickly to the boil, then add whatever fish they have to hand, putting the tougher fish into the pot first. Then they cook until all the fish is tender. Very good and very simple.

Croutons are small squares of bread fried until crisp in very hot fat, preferably butter.

Bean Soup

Fasolada

450g (1lb) cannellini beans
3.4 litres (6 pints) water
Chopped celery to taste
2 tablespoons tomato purée
2 large onions

2 large, chopped carrots
Handful chopped fresh parsley
125ml (4fl oz) olive oil
Salt and pepper to taste

Soak the beans overnight, then rinse them thoroughly in a colander under running water. Put them into a pan with the water and bring to the boil. Throw away this water, add the same quantity again, bring once more to the boil, reduce the heat, add the remaining ingredients and continue to cook slowly until the beans are very soft.

Some Greek cooks prefer to rub the soup through a sieve, others are emphatic that this is not necessary. The beans they insist, should be soft but whole.

Fasolada is the national dish of Greece, it is also considered to be a poor man's dish since beans are very cheap.

Beef and Pasta Soup

Soupa Pasta

2.3 litres (4 pints) beef stock
Celery and leaves to taste
Chopped fresh parsley to taste

225g (8oz) soup pasta (such as tiny
  stars, alphabet or other shapes)
Salt and pepper to taste

Bring the stock to the boil, remove any surplus grease or scum, add the remaining ingredients, except the pasta, and cook slowly until the stock is well-flavoured. Strain, bring again to the boil and add the pasta. Continue cooking until tender, about 10 minutes.

Cabbage Soup

Soupa Lahana

900g (2lb) finely shredded cabbage
2.3 litres (4 pints) water
Olive oil for frying
450g (1lb) peeled and
chopped tomatoes
1 tablespoon chopped fresh parsley

1 large, finely chopped onion
Croutons
Salt and pepper to taste
Butter for frying

First make the croutons. Cut some stale bread into small cubes and fry these in hot butter until brown and crisp. Remove at once, drain and put aside until required. About 1 tablespoon per plate is enough.

Lightly fry the onion in a little oil, add the water, bring this to the boil, then add the cabbage, tomatoes, salt and pepper. Bring again to the boil, lower the heat and cook slowly until the cabbage is tender. Just before serving sprinkle with parsley and add the croutons.

Finely chopped fresh aniseed can be added to this thick and nourishing winter soup. Crisp white cabbage is the best for soup making but other types of cabbage can be used.

Greek cooking

Easter Soup

Mayieritsa

The Greek Orthodox Church imposes severe Lenten fasting upon its communicants, forbidding all animal products, including eggs, butter and cheese. Nowadays fewer Greeks fast for the whole thirty days but even the most sophisticated fast during Holy Week. By the time Holy Week arrives there is a feeling of tension in the air, for the Greeks, intensely emotional, seem almost to relive the tragic anniversary of the happenings in Jerusalem nearly 2,000 years ago. Good Friday is a real day of mourning and even Athens, probably the noisiest city in the world, is quiet. Then, almost miraculously, in the evening of Holy Saturday the city reawakens to celebrate with bands and flags, with feasting and ceremony, the *'Proti Anastasis'* (The Resurrection) at midnight. Everyone, literally everyone, goes to the churches and cathedrals in villages and towns throughout the Greek archipelago to hear their priests and archbishops pronounce in ringing, dramatic tones, *'Christos Anesti'*, (Christ is risen). Everyone takes up the cry *'Christos Anesti'* and breaks a scarlet egg, which is carried in their pockets or handbags, bells clang, fireworks explode and rockets soar through the sky, even factory sirens wail, to announce the glad tidings. Athens's famed Constitution Square and the Acropolis are floodlit and thousands of people throng the streets laughing and wishing all and sundry *'Kalo Pascha'* (Happy Easter). Finally they slowly wend their ways home, everyone carrying a white candle, to crack more traditional scarlet-dyed eggs and to eat their Easter Soup. This is made from the feet, entrails and other odd bits of the lamb which is to be roasted and eaten on Easter Sunday.

Here are two recipes to make Easter Soup.

No. 1

The tripe, intestines, heart,
feet and liver of a lamb
50g (2oz) clarified butter
Handful finely chopped dill
Handful finely chopped parsley
6 spring onions

100g (4oz) rice
Juice 2 lemons
1 teaspoon flour
Salt to taste
Egg and Lemon Sauce
(see page 165)

Thoroughly clean all the meat, cut the tripe into 4 or 5 pieces and turn the intestines inside out. Scald the feet and the tripe, change the water (you need about 4.5 litres (8 pints)) and bring this to the boil; add salt and flour mixed with a little water to a paste. Cook gently for about 40 minutes.

Meanwhile soak for 30 minutes the remaining intestines, heart, etc, in cold, lemon-flavoured water. Drain and add to the feet and tripe. Continue cooking. In another pan heat the butter and fry the herbs and onions until the fat disappears, then stir this mixture into the soup. Continue to cook until the meat is quite tender, strain the soup through a sieve, return it to the pan and bring once more to the boil. Add the rice, cook until tender, stir in the Egg and Lemon Sauce, bring once more slowly to the boil, put aside for 5 minutes, then serve very hot.

No. 2.

A somewhat simpler version.

Into a large saucepan with plenty of water put about a pound of lamb bones with meat attached, a lamb's heart and 225g (8oz) of lamb's intestines tied in a bundle. Cook slowly until you have a good stock. Remove the bones, intestines and heart. Strip off the meat from the bones, slice the heart and return both to the pan. Add 225g (8oz) of chopped lamb's liver, some chopped spring onions, plenty of salt, pepper, a little chopped celery, chopped parsley, dill to flavour and lastly 50 or 75g (2 or 3oz) of rice. Cook fairly rapidly until the rice is soft. Remove the pan from the heat, add Egg and Lemon Sauce, stir for a few minutes over a low heat, cover and put aside for 5 minutes before serving.

Both recipes are sufficient for 6 or 8 people.

Greek cooking

Egg and Lemon Soup

Soupa Avgolemono

2.3 litres (4 pints) chicken stock
75g (3oz) long-grain rice
3 eggs

Salt
Juice 1 large lemon

Bring the stock to the boil, add salt if required. Throw in the rice and cook this until tender, about 15 minutes.

Whilst the soup is cooking prepare an Egg and Lemon Sauce. Beat the eggs well, then gradually beat in the lemon juice and, very slowly, 450ml (3/4 pint) of hot broth. Just before serving the soup add the sauce, stirring all the while. Simmer until the soup is again hot, cover and let it stand for 5 minutes on the side of the stove.

This soup has become probably one of the best known of the Greek soups and is a favourite throughout the Balkans. I have given the full directions for making the Egg and Lemon Sauce in this recipe because it is so much part of it.

Tripe Soup

Patsa

900g–1.4kg (2–3lb) tripe
2–3 cloves chopped garlic
Rind 1/2 lemon

Salt and pepper to taste
Egg and Lemon Sauce
(see page 165)

Cut open the tripe and wash it thoroughly, scraping the inside until perfectly clean. Put it into a saucepan, cover with cold water, add salt and bring slowly to boiling point. Pour away the water. Cut the tripe into small pieces and with 3.4 litres (6 pints) of water, the lemon rind, salt and pepper bring once to the boil, then simmer until tender, about 2 hours. Skim off the fat. Take out the tripe and cut it into even smaller pieces, return these to the stock (which is better if passed swiftly through a strainer) and bring this once more to the boil. Reduce the heat and simmer it gently. You may have to add more water or boiling broth, it depends on how many people are to eat the soup.

Just before serving add the Egg and Lemon Sauce in the usual way.

Any kind of tripe can be used for this soup, and scraps of celery, onions and other vegetables are often cooked with it to give additional flavour and strength, or what my mother used to call 'body'.

Lentil Soup

Fakasoupa

450g (1lb) yellow lentils
Chopped celery, carrots and
   onion to taste
1–2 finely chopped cloves garlic

1 bay leaf or pinch marjoram
Salt and pepper to taste
2–3 tablespoons malt vinegar

Clean the lentils and cook them for about 1 hour. Strain and return them to the pan with the remaining ingredients, except the vinegar, and at least 3.4 litres (6 pints) of fresh water. Bring this to the boil, then simmer until all the vegetables are very soft. Just before serving add the vinegar and stir this well into the soup. Continue to cook for another 5 minutes.

A bacon bone or some bacon rinds added to the soup (removed, of course, before serving) greatly improves the flavour.

Sweet Corn Soup

Soupa Apo Aravosito

This is a popular village soup from the island of Crete made from dried sweet corn. The corn is pounded and mixed with dried milk and kept during the winter. When required it is mixed with water and cooked. Its consistency is a matter for each cook to decide.

Greek cooking

Tomato Soup

Domato Soupa

Generally speaking, in Greece tomato soup is made from the juice of fresh tomatoes, but when these are not in season, from tomato paste. The tomato juice or paste is boiled with water, 50ml (2fl oz) of olive oil is added, to approximately 1.2 litres (2 pints) of water and plenty of salt and pepper. When the soup has been boiling for a few minutes 2 tablespoons of rice or noodles per person is added. Naturally, stock may be used instead of water. The quantity of paste or tomato juice used depends on individuals, but to 1.2 litres (2 pints) of water at least 1 good tablespoon of paste should be added, or about 300ml (1/2 pint) of fresh tomato juice, or even double the quantities.

A tin of tomato soup can be much improved by using it in this way.

Pasta Soup

Trahana Soupa

Trahana is not exactly pasta but this is probably the nearest translation of the word. This soup looks rather like a dish of porridge and is a speciality of the village cooks of Asia Minor. The favourite time to prepare *trahana* is in August when the goat's milk is at its best and the wheat has been brought in. The *trahana* dough is made by the peasants from goat's milk and wheat and is thick enough to break off into small pieces which are then rounded and shaped into balls, about the size of a hazel nut. These are then dried and rubbed between the hands until the dough is like a fine oatmeal. This is dropped into boiling broth, preferably chicken, and slowly cooked. Sometimes Egg and Lemon Sauce (see page 165) is added. Those who cannot afford a chicken make their soup simply from *trahana* and water.

Both peasants and fishermen like to take a bowl of *trahana* soup before starting off on their day's work. On their return in the evening they will take another bowl but, if they can afford it, they will add a glass or two of red wine to the pot first.

Vermicelli Soup

Fides Soupa

Almost any kind of stock may be used for this kind of soup and it can be either thick or thin. During Lent vermicelli soup should be made with water.

Brown 1 large, finely chopped onion in either butter or oil, then stir in enough tomato paste to flavour. Add 1.7 litres (3 pints) of vegetable stock (or water), salt and pepper. Bring to the boil then add as much vermicelli as you like. Just before the soup is served, add an Egg and Lemon Sauce (see page 165).

A simpler method of making this soup is to boil about 1.7 litres (3 pints) of stock, add salt, pepper and tomato paste to flavour and bring to a bubbling boil. Add as much vermicelli as you like, cook this until tender and then add the Egg and Lemon Sauce.

All varieties of macaroni may be used in this way as well. There is as much variety of pasta in Greece as there is in Italy. In fact, it is frequently claimed that the Greeks eat more pasta than the Italians and I am inclined to believe this. Stars, rounds, oblongs, lengths, all shapes of pasta are thrown into steaming bowls of broth, plus plenty of tomatoes, onions, garlic and chopped herbs. All this is finished off with the inevitable Egg and Lemon Sauce. Very simple and very good.

Greek cooking

Fish
Psaria

The Greeks have always been fond of fish, it is part of their staple diet, and that there should be plenty of good fish in Greece is not surprising since the mainland is practically surrounded by water and much of the country consists of hundreds of little islands.

In days gone by the arrival of the fresh catch was heralded by the tolling of a bell in all seaport towns. The catch of those days, I think, had more variety than today's, for, with the discovery of dynamite, there has been much indiscriminate fishing in Mediterranean waters. I remember when living in Beirut I could buy imported cold storage fish from Britain far cheaper than I could the local fish, which at times was nonexistent. This seemed to me ridiculous, as we had the sea at our doorsteps.

The Greeks eat varieties of shellfish such as sea urchins, sea quinces, etc, but although they have oysters they seldom seem to eat them because, they say, the oyster is a dirty eater. But it should be recorded that it is to the Greeks we owe the discovery of the oyster as an edible fish. At least so legendary history tells. One day, many centuries ago, a young Athenian boy was wandering along the beach in search of shells. Suddenly he espied an oyster in the act of yawning. Curious, he picked up the half-open shellfish and put his finger inside the shell. The indignant oyster at once snapped the shell together, causing the boy to give a sharp cry of pain and quickly withdraw the injured finger which he at once popped into his mouth. The flavour was delicious, so delicious that he broke open the shell, and swallowed the unfortunate oyster. And, we must suppose, he rushed home to tell his family of his great discovery. Since that fatal day the oyster has been a much harassed shellfish.

The favourite Greek way of cooking fish is to grill it, otherwise it is mixed with various types of vegetables, especially onions and tomatoes, and either baked or slowly simmered. I think that the cook would find many of these fish dishes quite simple and they do have the advantage of usually being served in the dish in which the fish is cooked.

Red Mullet Baked in Parchment

Barbounia Sto Harti

900g (2lb) red mullet
Olive oil
Lemon juice
Marjoram or thyme to taste

Lemon slices
Finely chopped parsley
Greaseproof paper
Salt and pepper

Clean the fish and rub it with olive oil. Cut the greaseproof paper into sizes to fit the fish and brush each piece with oil. (Remember each fish is to be wrapped separately.) Beat about 4 tablespoons each of the olive oil and lemon juice together, adding salt and pepper, and one of the herbs, it does not matter which. Put 1 fish on each piece of the paper and on top of the fish arrange 1 or 2 slices of lemon. Spoon the oil and lemon mixture over the fish. Fold the paper carefully so that none of the flavour of the fish escapes while it is cooking. (The package can be fastened with paper clips for extra security.) Place the packages in a baking pan, brush them with oil and bake at 190°C/375°F/Gas 5 until the fish is tender, about 25 or 30 minutes.

Larger fish can also be cooked in this manner, allow 15 minutes for each pound of fish.

Grilled Mullet

Barbounia Sti Shara

Thoroughly clean and wash as many mullet as required. Put them into a colander, sprinkle with salt and pepper and leave for 15 minutes. Put half a lemon on the end of a fork and pour some olive oil into a saucer, this is for basting the fish. Heat the grill, arrange the fish on a grid above or below the grill, dip the cut face of the lemon into the olive oil and frequently baste or rub the mullet with this to prevent the skin from bursting or becoming dry.

Serve the mullet with a lemon and olive oil dressing.

Greek cooking

Fried Mullet

Barbounia Tiyanita

Thoroughly clean and wash as many mullet as required. Put them in a colander, sprinkle with salt and lemon juice and leave for 15 minutes. Lightly coat with flour, then fry in hot olive oil until brown on both sides.

This is almost the national fish dish of Greece.

Savoury Mullet

Barbounia Savore

1.8kg (4lb) red mullet
600ml (1 pint) Tomato Sauce
  (see page 169–170)
Garlic, bayleaves and rosemary

Olive oil for frying
25g (1oz) plain flour
3 tablespoons white wine vinegar or
  dry white wine

Clean the fish, keeping on the heads and tails. Heat the oil, do not use too much, and fry the fish until brown on both sides. Take them from the pan and put into a serving dish deep enough to take some sauce. Pour off all but about 1 tablespoon of the oil, reheat the oil that is left in the pan and stir in the flour. When this is brown, add the Tomato Sauce, the vinegar or wine, finely chopped garlic (to taste), a little rosemary and 1 or 2 bayleaves. Simmer the sauce for 5 minutes, then pour it over the fish. Serve cold.

Fish Roe Rissoles

Taramo Keftethes

At one time I met two Greek-American girls who were staying in the same house with me in Athens and who insisted that some Greek-American recipes should be in any book of Greek cooking. The following recipe is one which they gave me. It can be made with the roe of the grey mullet, or cod's roe.

175g (6oz) fish roe	*1 tablespoon chopped fresh parsley*
2 large potatoes, mashed	*Salt and pepper*
1 small onion, grated	*Flour*
1 tablespoon chopped fresh mint	*Olive oil for frying*

Steep the roe for 10 minutes in boiling water, then remove and discard the membranes. Mash the roe with a fork, add the potato, onion, parsley, mint, salt and pepper and blend thoroughly with the roe. Shape into rissoles, roll in flour and fry in deep boiling oil until brown and crisp on the outside and soft inside.

Extremely popular in Greece, especially during Lent.

Greek cooking

Mayonnaise of Fish, Athens Style

Psari Mayonnaisa

This is simply boiled or steamed white fish, boned and broken into small pieces, with all the skin removed. It is then remoulded into its original shape, or as near to it as possible, and thickly covered with mayonnaise. The usual garnishings are sliced gherkins, green olives and thick slices of fresh cucumber. The quality of this dish depends entirely on the flavour of the fish and the mayonnaise (see page 170).

Usually when Greeks boil fish they add to the water 2 or 3 onions, the same quantity of carrots, a stalk or so of celery with the leaves, and usually 2 or more tomatoes. This stock is strained and served as a soup, the fish follows surrounded by the vegetables. To give variety the stock is sometimes flavoured with an Egg and Lemon Sauce (see page 165) but if you do not care for fish soup followed by fish, then the stock can be utilised the following day. In any case it should not be thrown away nor should the fish be cooked in plain salted water.

Baked Fresh Sardines with Lemon and Marjoram

Psari Riyanato

1.4–1.8kg (3–4lb) fresh sardines	Marjoram
Juice 2–3 lemons	Salt
25ml (8fl oz) olive oil	

Clean the sardines and arrange them in a fairly large baking dish. Beat the oil and lemon juice together until well blended and pour over the fish. Add salt and marjoram to taste and bake at 190°C/375°F/Gas 5 until tender, not more than 15 minutes.

If fresh sardines are not available, other small fish can be cooked in the same manner but not tinned sardines.

Fish as Prepared in the Island of Spetsai

Psari Fournou Spetsiotiko

1.8kg (4lb) any firm white fish
450ml (3/4 pint) olive oil
2 tablespoons tomato purée
Handful chopped fresh parsley

1–2 cloves chopped garlic
Salt and pepper to taste
Breadcrumbs
Lemon juice

Clean the fish, rub it well with salt and lemon juice, then arrange it in a baking dish. Put the oil and the remaining ingredients (except breadcrumbs) into a bowl and blend as for a sauce.

Pour most of the sauce over the fish and cover with half of the breadcrumbs. Take the remainder of the sauce and pour this over the breadcrumbs. Add the remaining breadcrumbs to make a top layer (this is done to produce a thick crust). Bake for about 1 hour at 190°C/375°F/Gas 5, basting the fish from time to time in its own sauce. If the fish should seem too dry, add some hot water, or, better still, white wine, but only a little sauce should be left by the time the fish is ready.

Greek cooking

Baked Fish with Tomatoes

Psari Fournou

1.8kg (4lb) white fish	Finely chopped fresh parsley
1.4kg (3lb) finely chopped tomatoes	150ml (¹/4 pint) olive oil

This is a simple dish. Clean the fish, arrange it in a baking dish, add the olive oil and cover with the tomatoes. Sprinkle with parsley and bake at 190°C/375°F/Gas 5 until tender.

Slices of potatoes can be added and the fish may be either all of one kind or well and truly mixed. If you let the fish remain covered by the tomatoes for an hour or two before cooking there is a considerable improvement in the flavour.

In Crete, where I lunched one day with the peasant caretaker of a girls' school, I was offered an extremely pleasant but simple dish of baked mixed fish of the cheapest kind. It had been prepared as above except that plenty of sliced onion had been added and also small potatoes surrounded the dish.

Palamida Cooked with Tomatoes

Palamitha Plari

Plaki is an all-embracing term and means any fish which is baked or braised with vegetables. Palamida is a large silver fish, very fat with a rich and heavy flesh, much of which is not quite white and often streaked with brown. It comes from Africa to the Black Sea where it lays its eggs before returning to Africa again. It swims the surface of the ocean and returns to Greek waters via the Dardanelles in shoals of billions from November to December. It is not generally considered an elegant fish but many discerning eaters (including myself), like it very much, especially when pickled and served as a *mezé*, as in Istanbul. In this recipe, if palamida is not available use any similar fish: cod, whiting or fresh haddock.

900g–1.4kg (2–3lb) fish	3 large sliced tomatoes
50ml (2fl oz) olive oil	2 cloves garlic
2 finely chopped onions	Juice 1 lemon
2–3 thickly sliced potatoes	Handful finely chopped fresh parsley
2–3 chopped stalks celery	1.2 litres (2 pints) water
2–3 sliced carrots	Salt and black pepper

Heat the olive oil in a shallow pan and fry the onions until they are brown. Boil the water and slowly add this to the onions and simmer until these are soft. Chop the garlic and add this with the prepared vegetables to the pan. Season with salt and pepper and cook for about 10 minutes. Clean the fish and cut it into pieces, any size you like. Arrange these on top of the vegetables. Add the parsley and sprinkle generously with lemon juice. Continue to cook for about 15 minutes or until the fish is tender. Arrange the fish in the centre of a platter and surround it with the vegetables.

Greek cooking

Fish Baked with Tomatoes, Onions and Black Olives

Psari Plari Tou Fournou

1 large fish, about 1.8kg (4lb)
4 large sliced tomatoes
2 large sliced onions
12 stoned black olives
150ml (¹/4 pint) dry white wine

1 sliced lemon
225ml (8fl oz) olive oil
Salt and pepper
Chopped fresh parsley, to taste

Wash and thoroughly clean the fish, remove the head and tail (the last is optional), and rub the fish with salt, pepper and lemon. Brush a baking tin with olive oil, cover with a layer of onion and tomato then add the fish, the remaining onion and tomato, the parsley and the olives. Pour in remaining olive oil and wine and arrange remaining slices of lemon down the length of the fish. Bake at 190°C/375°F/Gas 5 for about 40 minutes, longer cooking will not hurt the fish unless it becomes too dry.

Braised Mackerel

Scoubri Plaki

Clean and fillet 4 mackerel, then cook them in boiling water for 2 or 3 minutes. Leave until cold, then remove the bones. Do not discard the liquid.

Heat about 90ml (3fl oz) of olive oil and fry 4 sliced onions in this until brown. Lay half the onions at the bottom of a saucepan, add a handful of chopped fresh parsley and the oil from the pan. On top place the filleted mackerel, cover with the remaining onions and chopped fresh parsley to taste. Add 125ml (4fl oz) of dry white wine or wine vinegar and about 900ml (1 ¹/2 pints) of the liquid in which the mackerel was precooked. Add salt and pepper to taste, cover and cook over a moderate heat for about 15 minutes. Quite often peeled and sliced tomatoes are added, or a tablespoon of tomato purée.

Baked Fish with Black Olives

Psari Plari Me Elies

900g (2lb) fish
4 chopped tomatoes
4 finely chopped large onions
8 black olives

1–2 cloves chopped garlic
Salt and pepper
125–225ml (4–8fl oz) olive oil

If using large fish, cut it into rather thick steaks. Smaller fish, such as red mullet, can be used whole.

Clean the fish and place it in an oiled baking dish. Heat remaining oil in a frying pan, add the onions and garlic and fry until a light brown. Add tomatoes and continue cooking until these are fairly soft. Cover the fish with this mixture, add salt and pepper, about 50ml (2fl oz) of water and cook at 190°C/375°F/Gas 5 for 30 minutes. Stone the olives and add these about 5 minutes before the fish is ready.

More olives may be used, up to a dozen or so, and white wine instead of water.

Fish Cooked in Paper

Palamitha Sto Harti

Chop off the head, clean and wash the fish, then rub it in salt and lemon juice. Rub a fairly large piece of greaseproof paper with olive oil, place the fish on this, wrap it securely, and put the package into a baking dish. Rub the paper again with olive oil, and bake the fish at 190°C/375°F/Gas 5 for about 30 minutes or according to its size, remembering 10 minutes baking to every 450g (1lb) of fish.

Remove the paper, or better still undo the package, slide the fish on to a plate and then fillet it. Put the fillets on to a serving platter and cover with an oil and lemon dressing. Serve hot or cold.

For *palamida* see page 35.

Greek cooking

Fish Baked in Onion Sauce

Psari Me Saltsa Kremithia

1 fish, about 1.4kg (3lb)
2 large onions
3 large peeled and sliced
   tomatoes
1 tablespoon lemon juice

Olive oil
Handful finely chopped fresh parsley
Salt and pepper
Capers to taste (optional)
1.2 litres (2 pints) boiling water

Peel the onions and cut them into thick slices. Put these into a pan with the boiling water, salt and pepper to taste and the lemon juice. Cook until the onion is quite tender.

Clean the fish and cut it into thick slices, remove as many bones as possible without actually filleting it. Cook for 10 minutes with the onions. Take the fish from the pan and arrange it in a casserole, cover with tomatoes, parsley, capers (optional) and the olive oil. Add all the onion and enough of the onion liquid to just cover, then bake at 190°C/375°F/Gas 5 until the fish is tender. Serve hot. Enough for 6 people, if allowing 225g (8oz) of fish per person.

Almost any kind of white fish is suitable for this method of cooking fish, especially cod or haddock.

Baked Fish (With Onions and Garlic)

Psari Sto Fourno

1 large fish, about 1.8kg (4lb)
Juice 1 lemon
2 large finely chopped onions
3 cloves chopped garlic
125ml (4fl oz) olive oil
1 lemon, sliced

125ml (4fl oz) hot water
2 tablespoons finely chopped
 fresh parsley
Marjoram to taste (optional)
Salt and pepper

Clean the fish and split it down the centre. Rub inside with salt, pepper and lemon and leave for 30 minutes, then drain. Place it in a baking dish and add the water. Fill the inside with parsley and marjoram. Heat the olive oil and lightly fry the onions and garlic until the onions begin to soften but not brown. Pour this mixture over the fish, oil as well, arrange the slices of lemon down the length of the fish and bake at 190°C/375°F/Gas 5 until the fish is tender, about 1 hour, but the time varies according to the size of the fish. Basting from time to time is necessary.

This is unusual as Greeks generally do not stuff their fish.

Baked Fish in a Wine Sauce

Psari Fournou Me Krassi

1 large fish, about 1.8kg (4lb)
Salt and pepper
Olive oil

450ml (3/4 pint) tepid water
450ml (3/4 pint) dry white wine
2 teaspoons English mustard

Make a slit in the fish large enough to clean it inside and out but do not remove the head and tail. Rub inside and out with salt and pepper and place it in an oiled baking pan. Add the water and the wine, and the mustard mixed with a little water or wine to a thin paste.

Bake at 190°C/375°F/Gas 5 until the fish is tender, basting from time to time. If the sauce is reduced too much before the fish is cooked, add a little more wine. Allow 10 minutes' cooking for each 450g (1lb) of fish and if it is lean, gash the skin in 2 or 3 places to keep it from bursting.

Greek cooking

Grilled Fish

Psito Psari

Despite the Greek preference for cooking fish with olive oil and tomatoes they are also very fond of all kinds of grilled fish, particularly when grilled over charcoal. In the *tavernas* cooks are often apt to lay the fish directly on top of their huge woodburning stoves, a method which produces a rather dried out result. This is then gleefully counteracted by a basinful of olive oil poured over the fish. This is not one of my favourite methods of cooking fish but I do like charcoal-grilled fish.

Clean (but leave the heads and tails on) as many fish as required and sprinkle each inside and out with lemon juice, salt and pepper. Leave for about 30 minutes, the Greek cook usually leaves the fish in a colander. Put one half of a lemon on the end of a fork and some olive oil into a saucer. To barbecue the fish, place on a grid over glowing charcoal, alternatively cook under the grill. Brush it from time to time with the lemon dipped in oil. Carefully turn when brown and repeat the operation. Serve the fish immediately.

Many Greek cooks, especially *taverna* cooks, prefer to make a dressing from olive oil and pour this over the fish as soon as it is grilled, then leave it for 10 minutes or more. This means that the fish is served lukewarm, a fact which does not disturb the Greeks one iota but which causes tremendous stir among most foreigners. I prefer my fish either hot or cold but I did find after a while, as I became more used to the pattern of *taverna* life, that I did not mind lukewarm fish so much. However, I admit it took quite a while to get me to this state of grace.

Grilled fish is always served with small wedges of lemon.

Mackerel

Scoubri

Cut off the heads and clean as many mackerel as required. Sprinkle with plenty of salt and leave for 1 hour. Rub a grill pan or wire rack well with olive oil, lay the mackerel on top of this and grill gently or barbecue. Turn to brown the other side. When the fish are cooked right through (unless it is a large fish they are usually cooked through when browned on both sides) garnish with chopped fresh parsley and sliced raw onion rings and generously sprinkle with lemon. Serve hot.

Fish Steaks

Filleta Psariou

Rub the fish steaks or slices with salt. Cover a grill pan or wire rack with fresh bayleaves, and lay the fish on it. Gently grill or barbecue. Turn with care and when browned on both sides sprinkle with lemon juice, or serve with Garlic Sauce with Almonds (see page 166). The fish is done when it flakes easily with a fork.

Cod Steaks

Filleta Bakaliaros

Rub the fish steaks with salt and sprinkle with flour. Rub a grill pan or wire rack with olive oil and lay the fish on top. Gently grill or barbecue, turning the fish to brown on both sides. Cover the bottom of a platter with finely chopped fresh parsley and sliced raw onions and place the grilled slices of fish on top. Garnish with wedges of lemon.

Greek cooking

Snapper

Tsipoura

This fish is considered one of the best in Greece, it has a white flesh and not too many bones. It is often grilled, first being rubbed with oil and lemon and then very slowly cooked on both sides.

I remember the first time I ate *tsipoura*. My hostess pointed at the choicest portions then, from time to time, to make quite sure I missed nothing, she would dig out bits of the flesh for me and almost push this into my mouth, and with each piece I ate came an oration on the especial merit of this or that minute section of what I must agree was an excellent grilled fish.

Grilled Fish with Marjoram

Psari Me Riyani

1 large fish, about 1.8kg (4lb), cleaned
Lemon juice
Olive oil

Salt and pepper
Marjoram

The fish can be either whole or in fillets. Rub well with salt and pepper, brush with oil, sprinkle with lemon juice and marjoram to taste. If whole, retain heads and tails but clean thoroughly.

Grill the fish by whatever means you have until it begins to brown, baste with lemon juice, brush with oil, turn and repeat this on the other side, and turn again once or twice, until the fish is cooked through. If fillets are used you need only to turn once. Serve hot, sprinkled with a little freshly chopped marjoram and wedges of lemon.

A rather bitter type of salad, sometimes made with spinach, is often served with grilled fish in Greece. Otherwise a lettuce or watercress salad is the best.

Even nicer, according to Greek taste, is a salad of wild *radikia*, which is a type of wild radish found in the mountains. They have a bitter flavour, far removed in taste from the cultivated variety, and are 7.5–10 cm (3–4in) long with curly leaves.

Fried Fish with Sauce

Psari Me Saltsa

1.8kg (4lb) fish
Plain flour

Olive oil for frying
Salt and pepper

The fish for this type of preparation can either be cut into thick slices or steaks or, if small, kept whole. Heads and tails of whole fish are usually left on. Clean the fish, rub with salt and pepper, then roll in seasoned flour. Fry in boiling oil. When brown on one side, turn and brown the other. Take from the pan and keep hot while you make the sauce.

Saltsa

1 tablespoon tomato purée
2–4 cloves chopped garlic
1 bay leaf
125ml (4fl oz) hot water
Handful chopped fresh
  parsley (optional)

25g (1oz) plain flour
125ml (4fl oz) dry white wine
Pinch fresh rosemary (if liked)
Salt and pepper

Pour off most of the oil from the pan in which you have fried the fish, leaving just enough to fry the flour for a full 5 minutes, stirring all the while.

Dilute the tomato purée with the hot water, stir this into the flour, add salt, pepper, bay leaf, garlic, parsley and rosemary and cook gently for 10 minutes, stirring continuously. Add the wine, stir this into the sauce and simmer for a further 15 minutes. Pour the sauce over the fish and serve hot.

Greek cooking

Fried Smelts

Marides Tiganates

Wash as many smelts as required and pat them dry, then lightly coat with flour. The easiest way is to put the fish into a bag with some flour and shake the bag. Heat some olive oil and fry the smelts until they are as crisp as a biscuit.

If the smelts are very small you throw a number of them into the oil together. If large, press 4 or 5 of them together by their tails and shape them like a fan before frying. Whitebait make an excellent alternative.

Dried Fish Salad

Tsiros Salata

Tsiros is a 15cm (6in) long silver fish, not unlike, I think, the Bombay duck before it is dried. Like Bombay duck it is dried and salted, but then held over burning paper until the outer skin blisters and breaks. The fish is then filleted and broken into pieces. These are mixed with oil and vinegar and left marinading for 30 minutes. It is drained before serving as an appetizer.

My Greek friends told me that when their cooks are burning, or rather blistering, the *tsiros* they are banished to the kitchen balconies as the smell is quite impossible.

Fried Salt Cod with Garlic Sauce

Bakaliaros Skorthalia

A recipe for those with a palate for strong flavours. Dried salt cod is available from delicatessens and specialist food shops.

900g–1.4kg (2–3lb) dried salt cod
Olive oil for frying

Plain flour
Skorthalia Sauce (see page 167).

Soak the fish in cold water for 12 hours, changing the water twice. Wash very thoroughly in cold water and remove the bones and skin. Dry and dip in flour and fry in hot deep olive oil until browned on both sides. Serve hot with a *skorthalia* sauce.

Boiled Salt Codfish

Bakaliaros Vrastos

900g (2lb) dried salt cod
10–12 small peeled onions
900g (2lb) small peeled
 potatoes

3–4 celery stalks, chopped
50–125ml (2–4fl oz) olive oil
Juice 1/2 small lemon
Pepper

Cut the fish into serving pieces and soak for 12 hours in cold water, changing it twice. Wash it and remove the skin. Drain and put into a pan with the onions, celery and potatoes. Cover with cold water. Whip the olive oil, lemon juice and pepper together and stir into the water. Cook very gently until the fish is tender, about 30 or 40 minutes.
 Serve with the vegetables and an oil and lemon dressing.

Greek cooking

Lobster with Mayonnaise

Astakos Vrastos Me Mayonnaisa

1 small lobster per person
Salt and chopped fresh parsley

125ml (4fl oz) vinegar
Mayonnaise Sauce (see page 170)

Plunge the live lobsters head first into a large pot filled with boiling, salted water flavoured with vinegar. Cook rapidly for 5 minutes, then lower the heat and cook for another 10 minutes. Cool them in water for 15 minutes. Dry with a cloth, break off the claws and carefully cut the lobster lengthways. Remove the dark vein along the back, and the small sac behind the head, lift the meat from the tail and cut this into thick pieces and arrange on a platter. Crack the claws and take out the meat, put this with the tail meat. Take out the coral and the green liver and mix with the mayonnaise.

Serve the lobster with a coating of mayonnaise, or even a simple oil and lemon dressing.

Braised Shrimps (or Prawns)

Yarides Me Saltsa

900g (2lb) unshelled shrimps
  (or prawns)
2 medium finely
  chopped onions
4 chopped tomatoes

2–3 tablespoons chopped fresh parsley
1 tablespoon tomato purée
Salt and pepper
50–125ml (2–4fl oz) olive oil

Wash the shrimps (or prawns) thoroughly and drain. Heat the oil in a large saucepan and fry the onions for about 5 minutes, add the purée and the chopped tomatoes and cook over a moderate heat for about 5 minutes. Add the parsley, salt, pepper and finally the shrimps. Cover and cook for 15 minutes or until the shells are a bright pink and easily removed. Take the shrimps from the pan (keep the sauce simmering) and, when cool enough to handle, quickly peel them and remove the black vein that runs down the back. Drop the shrimps back into the sauce. As soon as all the shrimps are back and just reheated, serve.

Octopus in Red Wine

Htapodi Krassato

Octopus, when it is good, has something of the flavour of lobster and can be much more tender. It all depends on the method of killing the creature, the usual way being a systematic slow beating against a rock or something equally hard and handy. I remember once, when staying in a small hotel along the coast just outside Athens, I heard every morning a slow thump, thump. Curious, I went down to the shore and saw men slapping grey masses of octopus against the flat rock. The octopus, I was told, dies hard and must be killed in this manner; the flesh can be very tough and it needs at least forty hearty slaps to make it tender. It is always the fisherman and not the cook who does all this beating or slapping and it is usual to kill the octopus as soon as the boats land. By the time they reach the shops or markets they are ready for cooking, although a little more hammering with a kitchen mallet does them no harm. Nowadays squid is more readily available and makes a good alternative to octopus.

1 octopus or cleaned squid
* weighing 900g (2lb)*
50ml (2fl oz) olive oil
2 finely chopped onions

450ml (3/4 pint) dry red wine
1/2 teaspoon pepper
1–2 celery stalks, chopped
1 bay leaf

Carefully clean the octopus, remove and discard the inkbag. Put the octopus or squid into a pan without adding any liquid and cook it over a moderate heat for 5–10 minutes. Remove the tentacles and cut these into pieces. Cut the remaining flesh into chunks, and peel off the skin (this peeling is optional, some Greeks do, some don't). Heat the olive oil and lightly fry the chopped onion until it changes colour, then add the remaining ingredients and the octopus or squid pieces. Simmer gently for about 3 hours. Stir occasionally and serve hot.

Greek cooking

Octopus Stewed in Onions

Htapodi Stifado Me Kremithia

900g (2lb) small octopus or
  cleaned squid
450g (1lb) sliced onions
125ml (4fl oz) good
  quality vinegar
125ml (4fl oz) dry white wine

150ml (¼ pint) tomato purée diluted
  with 4 tablespoons water
50ml (2fl oz) olive oil
Salt and pepper
1–2 cloves chopped garlic

Clean the octopus and remove the inkbag (some cooks keep the inkbag intact but this makes not only a very dark sauce but also gives a pretty strong flavour). Cook the octopus or squid for 5–10 minutes in a pan without adding any liquid. Chop off the tentacles and cut the body into strips of more or less equal size. Heat the oil and simmer the onions until they begin to soften but do not let them change colour. Add the garlic and the octopus or squid and continue simmering for 5 minutes before adding the vinegar, wine, salt, pepper and tomato purée. Cover the pan and cook slowly for 3 hours or until the octopus is really tender.

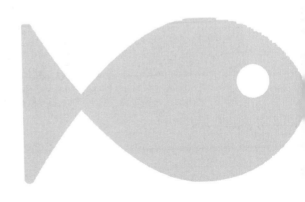

Squids

Kalamaria Yemista

These can be delicious when really small and tender and one of the side pleasures of drinking ouzo on the seashore is to eat these tiny squids which have been fried in deep oil, sometimes *au naturel*, sometimes dipped in egg and breadcrumbs. The important point is to get them served piping hot for, as I have already remarked, the Greeks are never troubled when their food is served lukewarm.

Larger squids are somewhat tougher and are better when they are stuffed.

12 squids	50–125ml (2–4fl oz) olive oil
Salt and pepper	125ml (4fl oz) thick tomato juice

Filling

125ml (4fl oz) olive oil	2 tablespoons chopped
3 large finely chopped onions	fresh dill or mint
100g (4oz) Basmati rice	1 heaped tablespoon pine nuts
4 tablespoons fresh chopped parsley	125ml (4fl oz) dry red wine

Wash the squids thoroughly, remove the inkbag, head and entrails. Cut off the feelers from the head and put these aside for later use. Season the bodies with salt and pepper. Mix the oil and tomato juice, drop the squids into this and leave them until required.

Filling. Heat the olive oil and lightly brown the onions. Cut the feelers into small pieces and add them to the pan, simmer until they change colour. Add the rice, parsley, dill (or mint) and nuts and cook for 5 minutes, stirring the mixture from time to time, preferably with a wooden spoon.

Partially fill the squids with the stuffing, not too full, for the rice has to swell. Close the openings either by rough sewing or with toothpicks. Arrange the squids in an oiled baking dish and then carefully pour a little of the wine into each. Pour over them the olive oil and tomato juice in which they have been marinating and enough boiling water to just cover. Bake at 190°C/375°F/Gas 5 for about 1 hour, or until the squids are tender and the sauce is thick. Preferably, according to the Greeks, served cold.

Greek cooking

Stuffed Mussels

Mithia Yemista

36 mussels
600ml (1 pint) boiling fish stock
  or water

4 tablespoons tomato purée
125ml (4fl oz) dry white wine
Salt and pepper

Filling

125ml (4fl oz) olive oil
100g (4oz) uncooked long-grain rice
4 large chopped onions
25–50g (1–2oz) pine nuts

50g (2oz) currants
Salt and black pepper
2 tablespoons chopped parsley

Scrub the shells with a stiff brush and wash them well. Open the mussels carefully without breaking or separating the shells. Remove and discard the beard and the black parts of the mussels, wash in several waters and then leave in cold water until required.

Filling. Heat the olive oil and fry the onions until a golden colour, add rice, cover and continue cooking for 20 minutes. Add the remaining ingredients and continue to cook for another 20 minutes, by which time all the liquid should be absorbed. Leave to cool. Fill each of the mussel shells with some of the stuffing, close the shells firmly and tie each one with thread. Pack the mussels tightly into a saucepan, pour in 600ml (1 pint) of water, the tomato purée (diluted with the wine), salt and pepper and cook slowly for 30 minutes. Leave to cool in the pan, drain off any remaining liquid, there will not be much. Remove the thread and serve the mussels cold with wedges of lemon. If preferred you can serve them hot. Either way they are extremely good.

Sea Urchins

Ahinoi

Sea urchins or, as some people call them, 'pin cushions of the sea' have long been a Mediterranean favourite. In England gourmets compare them with, say, caviare or *pâté de foie gras*.

Sea urchins are usually served as appetizers. The shell must be prised open, as one does with an oyster, and they are laid out on a plate, again in the manner of arranged oysters. The top half of the shell is discarded, the yellow roe (or edible ovaries) nestling inside the lower half of the shell is then sprinkled with a little lemon juice and olive oil. Served with buttered brown bread and white wine, they make a good beginning to any meal. In Greece, pedlars wander around the beaches with baskets of sea urchins and *kydonias*, another small shellfish, and perfectly delicious.

Greek cooking

Meat
Kreata

While the modern Greek means lamb when he talks of meat, and then goat and pork, the ancients talked much of beef. Homer sang of the delights of roast beef on which his men feasted. And one wonders whether Charles Lamb was right with his story of the first roast pig, for Aeschylus wrote long before Lamb, of sucking pig:

But I will place this carefully fed pig
Within the crackling oven; and, I pray,
What nicer dish can e'er be given to man?

I wonder whether those carefully fed pigs were peach fed like those of Hungary?

Although the Greeks still have their roasts baked in the oven, most of the best meat cooking of Greece is done on a spit, much the same kind of spit their ancestors used. With the introduction of the electric rotary spit, culinary art has been brought full circle. We started with the spit and we have come back to it. In days gone by small dogs and manpower rotated the mighty spits, today in Greece manpower still operates.

Looking into the history of spit cooking there is one story I like very much. It concerns the spit of the noble and opulent Count de Castel (not a Greek, I know) who had a spit which turned 130 different roasts at the same time. It also played twenty-four different tunes. For example, the fifth tune might announce that the chickens were ready, and at the tenth it was time to look at the turkey. The twelfth, perhaps, announced the sucking pig was done to a turn and so on. The cook, it is said, knew the exact note on which to grasp the roast as it turned slowly round and round.

Many of the meat recipes in this section are for spit roasting, and the vast majority can be used rather well with mutton, although the recipes call for lamb.

Meat in Greece is not butchered as in England and when Greeks go shopping they like to see carcasses hanging up bright and dripping, waiting for the butcher to hack off just the piece they want. This can be disconcerting for the cook used to simply asking for the cuts which the cookery book calls for, but it does help one's knowledge of animal anatomy.

Lamb Roast on a Spit

Arni

When a Greek talks of meat he usually means lamb. Following closely in his mind is milk-fed kid which, if killed before it is three weeks old or before it has been out to pasture, has a flesh as white and as delicate as a spring chicken. Mutton for the Greeks does not exist. It is old, it has an odour, it is in fact mutton.

Greeks, it is claimed, are either feasting or fasting. After they have fasted they like to make up for lost time. They try to eat lamb four times a year, at Christmas, when it is in the stage known as 'yearling lamb', quite large but still tender and juicy; in the first two weeks of carnival, when it is young and melting; on St George's Day, 23 April, and, most important, at Easter. At Eastertide the whole country, including all the hundreds of surrounding islands, is covered by a cloud of lamb-impregnated smoke. Starting in the early morning, from every nook and cranny you see the thin spirals of smoke rising from charcoal fires. In the country men sit gazing almost entranced beside the roasting pits, which are filled with charcoal, expertly turning the Easter roasting lamb on its spit. Often the charcoal is made from pine wood which gives a slight flavour of resin to the meat as it sputters and spits and the fat drops from the slowly revolving lamb into the smouldering charcoal.

A lamb is prepared the day before roasting. Although the lamb can be roasted in the home, Greeks in the country prefer their lamb to be cooked on a spit out of doors. In the towns, instead of tunnelling charcoal pits in the earth, special charcoal stoves of tin or other similar metal are made. The principle is the same: the bottom is filled with charcoal and a spit is built above on which the lamb is stretched. One end of the spit is made into a handle which can be turned like the cranking handle of a car, but with less effort.

Two things are important with the roasting of lamb. First, the fire must be regulated to give a uniform heat, and secondly, the lamb must be placed sufficiently far from the fire to prevent it from scorching. This distance is decreased as the roasting continues. The dripping pan below must contain a sufficient quantity of butter, flavoured with thyme and lemon juice. The spit is turned slowly and patiently for 3 hours and the lamb continually basted. The spit is then brought nearer and nearer to the fire as the lamb begins to turn a golden brown, so the heat is concentrated on the legs and shoulders. Less heat is required for the belly and head parts. Both these latter parts burn

continued

Greek cooking

easily and if cooked at the same heat as the fleshy parts will become dry while the rest will only be half cooked. The juice from the lamb is caught in the dripping pan.

Let me admit that roasting the Greek Easter lamb does require an experienced hand for it to become the delicacy it should be. Perfection has been achieved by the shepherds in the Greek mountains who know how to roast meat on a spit better than most people. And it is easy to see why. After St George's Day the shepherds must move with their flocks of sheep and goats to new pastures. They will be away from home and good food for a long while, during which time they live a frugal and meatless existence. So, before they leave, they are determined to have one last meat fling. It is no uncommon sight in the country, in April, to see the shepherds, man and boy, patiently roasting a lamb on a spit (savouring every smell) for a meal which in memory will last them for a period when their main items of diet will be rather hard, black bread, strongly flavoured goat's cheese and curds.

Those shepherds who do not stick to the mountains but yearn for the bright city lights have discovered a good source of income. They have opened up simple but appetizing lamb-roasting restaurants in the heart of Athens.

But it is not only in the mountains and in the heart of Athens that you can get a meal of lamb or other meat roasted on a spit. There are many tavernas throughout the country which prepare such food. I remember, in particular, driving along the coastal road below the dark hills of Delphi where I spotted a whole succulent yearling lamb being tenderly roasted. We decided that since it was lunch time we would eat then and there. The car was stopped and we stepped out under the pines to sit at a table set on the beach. The proprietor rushed up to John Hare, our host, and greeted him with an almost violent effusion of Greek which turned out to be a friendly welcome to an old friend. He quickly brought us ouzo and black olives, for this is the area of some of the finest and largest olive groves in Greece, and some white feta cheese, all this 'on the house'. We followed this with soft brown bread, tomato salad and finally tender chunks from the yearling lamb which the proprietor's wife was turning very slowly over glowing charcoal. By this time we had changed our drink to the local retsina wine which matched the scent of the pine trees. Soon our table was covered with plates of lamb, and although we protested that we simply could not eat another morsel we managed to deplete that lamb considerably. One or two other tables were taken up by excited Greeks who also took their toll of the meat. Another lamb, I was assured, would take its place for the evening customers, for our small taverna had a high local reputation. It was a very genuine taverna, its kitchen also the restaurant, although for most of the year clients could eat to their stomachs' content under the pines on the seashore.

Easter Lamb (for the town)

Arnaki Sti Souvla

Although the country people can prepare a whole Easter lamb in their front or back gardens, most people in Athens and the larger towns find this more difficult. This recipe is one which the cook can manage in any country where milk-lamb is available. You can use a joint of lamb, such as leg or shoulder, the result will be good but it will *not* be Easter Lamb.

Put the joint into a baking tin in a very hot oven to quickly sear. Baste generously with butter, reduce the heat and roast until the meat is about half tender. Add some half-cooked butter beans, or fresh broad beans, a fair quantity of small onions, and cover with stock. Add salt, pepper and garlic to taste. Continue roasting adding more hot stock if required.

Easter lamb can be cooked just as easily on top of the stove in a braising pan.

In Athens potatoes are often added when the meat is about half-cooked. In the days before home ovens were popular, every weekend during the lamb season, bakers' ovens, after the bread baking, used to be filled with tins of meat prepared in the above fashion.

Lamb Roasted in Paper

Arni Exotica

Food cooked in a paper wrapping is called *klephtes* in most parts of Greece and had its origin, so one hears, in the days of the Turkish occupation. The *klephtes*, or guerrilla bands, which roamed the mountains harassing the Turks, wrapped their food in this way in order that the aroma of food being cooked should not reach the nostrils of the Turkish guards. In the mountains the meat was heavily seasoned with mountain herbs (such herbs still reach the sophisticated shops of Athens today) wrapped in oiled paper, pushed into earthenware containers and cooked for hours among the smouldering

continued

Greek cooking

embers of pine logs and twigs. This recipe is for the urban version of *klephtes* cooking.

900g–1.4kg (2–3lb) shoulder
  lamb or a small leg
Salt, pepper and marjoram to
  taste
Plenty of garlic cut into slivers
Roughly 4 tablespoons olive oil

Juice 1 large lemon
About 50g (2oz) Kasseri
  (or Gruyère) cheese cut into cubes
4–6 pieces greaseproof
  paper large enough to hold
  individual portions

Wipe the meat clean then cut it into serving portions. Rub well with salt, pepper and marjoram (another similar herb will do as well), olive oil and lemon juice. Cut incisions into the meat and insert the garlic into these. Lightly oil the sheets of paper and arrange some of the meat on each piece. Top with cheese. Wrap carefully and fold the paper securely, twisting the ends tightly so that none of the juice escapes. Rub the packages with oil, place in a roasting pan and bake at 190°C/375°F/Gas 5 for about 3 to 4 hours. Serve in the paper.

This method of cooking lamb is popular in many of the Greek tavernas and the recipe varies according to the ideas of the Greek owner.

There are a couple of points about this kind of cooking which it is as well to know. The oven should really be moderate and when the packages are placed in the baking pan they should all just touch, that is, there should be no space left in between each package. No water, no oil, may be added; don't cover the pan and don't turn the packages. The cheese must always be on top of the meat and care must be taken that the paper does not scorch. So do not hurry the cooking. Serve piping hot in the paper to retain the piquant flavour of the meat.

For variety you can use less lamb and make up with chopped vegetables, such as squares of onion, aubergine, potatoes, a few peas and strips of green pepper.

900g (2lb) of meat is sufficient for 4 people.

Braised Lamb

Arni Kokkinisto

900g–1.4kg (2–3lb) diced lamb
75g (3oz) butter
1 large finely chopped onion
1 bay leaf

Garlic to taste
Salt and pepper
Stock or water
90ml (3fl oz) dry white wine

Melt the butter, either in a saucepan or a braising pan, add the meat, then when it is brown (or as the Greeks say, red) add the onion and continue frying until this is a light golden colour. Add the wine, rather gradually, then enough stock to just cover the bottom of the pan. Flavour with salt, pepper, garlic and the bay leaf. Cook over a medium heat until the meat is so tender that it will break easily with a fork.

Serve with any green vegetables, cauliflower or rice, or small new potatoes which can be put in with the meat 30 minutes or so before it is ready. The garlic can be rubbed into the meat if preferred and a handful of chopped fresh parsley may be added with the bay leaf.

Arni Kokkinisto really means 'red' lamb.

Greek cooking

Lamb with Tomatoes

Arni Me Domates

1.4kg (3lb) red lamb
6 large peeled and chopped
  tomatoes
300ml (¹/2 pint) hot water

Small piece cinnamon
75g (3oz) butter
Salt and pepper

Rub the meat liberally with salt and pepper. Leave for 30 minutes. Heat the butter in a frying pan, add the pieces of meat and let them brown. Transfer to a saucepan. Put the tomatoes into the frying pan, bring once to the boil, then cook gently until soft. Add the tomatoes to the meat, add salt, pepper and cinnamon and cook slowly until the meat is very tender. From time to time peer into the pan and if the meat shows signs of becoming too dry, gradually add boiling water. The meat should be neither dry nor swimming in sauce. Remove cinnamon before serving.

Can be served with rice, potatoes or any of the pasta family, such as noodles or spaghetti. Enough for 4–6 people.

Lamb Cooked with Beans

Arni Me Fassolia

A typical and simple dish. Butter beans are soaked overnight and next day cooked with cubes of lamb flavoured with chopped onions (sometimes first browned). When the meat and beans are almost cooked, some peeled and chopped tomatoes are added and slow cooking continued until the meat and beans are tender. Garlic is sometimes added.

The Greeks have a word for the type of white beans used in this recipe, it is 'giant'.

Lamb with Spinach and Egg and Lemon Sauce

Arni Me Spanaki Avgolemono

1.4kg (3lb) diced lamb
1.4kg (3lb) spinach
2 medium finely chopped onions
75g (3oz) butter

Salt and pepper
225ml (8fl oz) stock or water
Egg and Lemon Sauce
    (see page 165)

Heat the butter; when this is hot, add the onions and fry these until a light brown. Add the meat (stirring as you do so), salt and pepper and cook over a high heat for just 5 minutes, which will bring everything to the boil. Add the liquid, reduce the heat to almost simmering point and continue to cook until the meat is tender.

In the meantime clean and pick over the spinach, discarding any coarse leaves and the stems. Put into a saucepan over a medium heat and cook without water until the spinach is tender. Drain and remove the strong greenish liquid. Now put the drained spinach on top of the meat, cover and cook slowly for 15 minutes, moving the pan from time to time to prevent sticking. You may find that a little more liquid is required, if this is added it should be hot stock or water, but any extra liquid must be added with caution as this is meant to be a fairly dry dish. On the other hand, there must be just enough liquid left to add to the sauce. Just before serving add the Egg and Lemon Sauce and serve hot.

The Greeks usually cook dishes of this type in fireproof two-handled casseroles, which can be brought to the table and are also easy to handle, especially when shaking the pan is required.

Greek cooking

Baked Lamb with Tomatoes

Psito Arni Me Domates

Put a 900g (2lb) leg of lamb into a baking pan with butter, salt and pepper. Cover with peeled and sliced tomatoes. Sprinkle with oil and melted butter and bake at 150°C/300°F/Gas 2 until tender, about 2¹/2 hours if lamb is used, longer for mutton.

Lamb with Lettuce Hearts

Arni Me Maroulia

A Greek philosopher, Aristoxenus, called lettuce 'the green cakes that the earth has prepared'. It is said that he loved lettuces so much that he used to water them with the sweet wine of Chios.

Cut 900g (2lb) of leg or shoulder of lamb into pieces about the size of an egg. Put these into a pan with 2 or 3 tablespoons of olive oil or butter, add 4 finely chopped onions and simmer everything until most of the fat has been absorbed but neither the meat nor the onions have become brown. Add 25g (1oz) of flour, stir this into the meat and onions, then, still stirring, add hot stock or water to cover.

In the meantime, while the meat is simmering, steep 3 or 4 very small lettuce hearts in boiling water (dark or coarse leaves should be discarded) and add them to the meat, pressing them down slightly. Add some finely chopped fresh dill, salt and pepper and cook for another 15 minutes.

This dish can be served as it is or with Egg and Lemon Sauce (see page 164). If a sauce is added, take the pan from the heat, gently stir in the sauce and leave it to settle for a few minutes before serving, remembering, of course, to take a little of the liquid from the pan to put in the sauce.

Lamb with Artichokes and Egg and Lemon Sauce

Arni Me Anginares Avgolemono

900g (2lb) leg lamb	Lemon juice
1–2 chopped onions	Handful chopped fresh parsley
12 small globe artichokes	Egg and Lemon Sauce
50–75g (2–3oz) butter	(see page 165)
25g (1oz) plain flour	Salt and pepper

Wash and dry the lamb and chop it into small pieces. Snip off the stems of the artichokes and cut the heads in half, remove the choke and any coarse leaves. Trim each artichoke round the base, rub it with lemon juice and drop into cold water until required.

Heat the butter, lightly fry the onions, add the meat and simmer without browning either the meat or onions until all the butter has been absorbed. Add flour, stir this well into the meat and onions, then pour in enough water to a little more than cover. Bring to the boil, put the artichokes on top of the meat, add parsley, salt, pepper and 1 tablespoon of lemon juice. Cover and cook until the meat and artichokes are quite tender. Avoid stirring, for the artichokes might break and this spoils the appearance of the dish. When the meat is tender, add Egg and Lemon Sauce (taking some of the broth from the pan to make the sauce), simmer for 5 minutes, then leave covered but without heat for 5 minutes. Serve hot.

Tinned artichokes can be used in this recipe but they need very little cooking so add them to the meat when it is quite tender.

To serve this dish, first take out the artichokes and arrange them on a plate so that they surround the meat.

⊃ with Celeriac and
ıon Sauce

ıe Selino Avgolemono

g–1.4kg (2–3lb) diced lamb	Salt and pepper
ml (3fl oz) olive oil	Egg and Lemon Sauce
large finely chopped onion	(see page 165)
450g (1lb) celeriac or celery	

If using celeriac, this must be peeled and trimmed and cut into wedges; if using ordinary celery, clean and cut it into substantial pieces.

Heat the oil, lightly brown the meat, add the onion and cook over a medium heat for 5 minutes. Reduce the heat, add salt and pepper and hot water to cover. Continue to cook fairly slowly until the meat becomes tender, then add the celery and cook this until it is soft. Take the pan from the heat, stir in the sauce and do this carefully, otherwise the celery becomes too mashed, return the pan to the heat for 3 minutes, then leave covered for 5 minutes by the side of the stove. Serve hot.

Garlic may be added to this dish, for it adds flavour both to the meat and the celery. If using celeriac it must be added to the pan fairly soon after the meat for it takes some time to cook, at least 1 hour. Lamb with celery or celeriac is not frequent in Greece for the flavour of this vegetable is considered to go better with pork, a richer and fatter meat.

Lamb with Courgettes

Arni Me Kolokithia

1.4kg (3lb) leg lamb
2 chopped onions
6–8 courgettes
100g (4oz) butter

1–2 cloves chopped garlic
Handful finely chopped fresh parsley
4–6 small tomatoes
Salt and pepper

Wipe the meat with a damp cloth and cut it into egg-sized pieces. Melt 75g (3oz) of butter and gently fry the meat until just brown. Add the onions, fry these for a few minutes, then add the tomatoes, garlic, parsley, salt and pepper. Cook over a low heat for 1 hour or until tender. While the meat is cooking, very lightly scrape the skin off the courgettes and cut them into halves, or better still leave whole if small enough. Heat the remaining butter, slightly brown the courgettes, then add them to the simmering stew. Continue to cook gently for another 20 or 30 minutes or until the lamb is quite tender.

If a slightly less rich dish is preferred add the courgettes without first browning them. Other vegetables such as peas, cauliflower and small new potatoes can be cooked with lamb in this fashion.

Greek cooking

Lamb and Ladies' Finger Stew

Arni Kokinisto Me Bamies

Ladies' fingers or okra are the names given to a green vegetable grown in the tropics and in the pleasant climate of the Mediterranean. In shape a ladies' finger looks like, a lady's finger, and it has a rather gooey texture. It is also popular in America, especially in the deep south, and there it is called okra.

1.4kg (3lb) leg lamb, cut into
  serving pieces
700g (1½lb) ladies' fingers
600ml (1 pint) Tomato Sauce
  (see pages 70–1) or juice or soup

150ml (¼ pint) vinegar
75g (3oz) butter
Salt and pepper

Mix the vinegar with 600ml (1 pint) of cold water and in this soak the ladies' fingers for 30 minutes, turning them from time to time. Strain before using.

Heat the butter in a large saucepan, fry the pieces of meat until brown, turning them frequently. Add Tomato Sauce (juice or soup), salt and pepper to taste and simmer for 1 hour. Add the ladies' fingers and arrange these so that the meat remains in the centre of the saucepan. Continue cooking over a low heat until the meat is really tender and the ladies' fingers soft. Turn out to serve but try to keep the meat in the middle of the dish and the ladies' fingers surrounding it.

Lamb with French Beans

Arni Me Fassolia Fresca

1.4kg (3lb) diced lamb
900g (2lb) French beans
4 chopped tomatoes
1 large finely chopped onion

1–2 cloves chopped garlic
75g (3oz) butter
Salt and pepper
300ml (1/2 pint) boiling water

Top and tail the beans, then break each one into 2 or 3 pieces. Sauté the meat quickly in the melted butter and fry until brown. Transfer the meat to a saucepan and in the same fat fry the onion until a light brown. Add the tomatoes, garlic, salt and pepper and cook until the mixture is like a sauce. Pour this mixture over the meat, cover it and cook slowly until the meat is quite tender. Add the boiling water, then the beans, shake the pan and continue cooking for another 30 minutes.

Instead of diced lamb, this dish can be prepared with lamb chops, veal, pork chops or with beef.

Greek cooking

Lamb with Spaghetti

Arni Me Spageto

Meat with any of the pasta products is tremendously popular in all parts of Greece.

1.4kg (3lb) leg lamb
1 large finely chopped onion
450g (1lb) broken spaghetti
4 chopped tomatoes
1–2 cloves chopped garlic

1.2 litres (2 pints) hot water
1–2 tablespoons tomato purée
Salt and pepper
Grated Cheddar cheese (optional)

Clean the meat, cut it into cubes and put into a large baking tin. Add the tomatoes, tomato purée, onion, garlic, seasonings and 300ml (½ pint) of hot water. Bake at 190°C/375°F/Gas 5 until the meat is tender, add the remaining water and bring this to the boil. Add the spaghetti and continue to cook until this is tender, about 20 minutes. Stir the spaghetti and the meat together. Serve hot and, if liked, sprinkle with grated Cheddar cheese.

This can be cooked equally well on top of the stove.

Cutlets may be used instead of leg of lamb.

Roast Lamb with Noodles

Yiouvetsi

This is a speciality of several Athenian tavernas as well as of Greek cooks. In the Athenian winter, which can be very cold, the warm smell of the kitchens penetrates the eating section of the tavernas and the stomach takes kindly to a plate of *yiouvetsi*. Some tavernas prepare this in small individual earthenware dishes and bring it piping hot from the oven to the table. Then the waiter turns it out with one swift movement. This recipe is for a family *yiouvetsi* and is made in one large casserole or pot. It can be served from the casserole or turned out on to a large platter.

900g (2lb) leg or shoulder lamb cut into cubes	*450g (1lb) noodles or broken macaroni*
75g (3oz) butter	*About 600ml (1 pint) thick Tomato Sauce or soup*
2.3 litres (4 pints) hot meat stock or water	*Cheese (see below)*
	Salt and pepper

Put the lamb into a roasting tin or shallow casserole, sprinkle with salt and pepper and add the butter. Bake at 190°C/375°F/Gas 5 to brown. Turn the pieces from time to time. Add the Tomato Sauce or soup and 600ml (1 pint) of the meat stock or water. Continue baking until the meat is tender, stirring frequently. When the meat is really tender, take it from the pan and keep hot. Add the remaining stock to the pan, season to taste, then bring the liquid to the boil. Add the noodles or macaroni, cook these until they are tender and have absorbed all the liquid. Arrange the hot meat on a platter and smother it with the noodles. Or return the meat to the noodles and serve the *yiouvetsi* in the casserole. Garnish with some small squares of cheese. The Greeks use *Kasseri* cheese but if this is not available use a Gruyère or Cheddar.

Any type of pasta or rice can be cooked in this manner but actually macaroni is preferable, as the sauce fills the cavity of the macaroni and adds to its flavour.

Greek cooking

Lamb Fricassée with Egg and Lemon Sauce

Arni Fricasse Avgolemono

The Greeks have many kinds of fricassée dishes which are made with veal, lamb or beef. Lamb fricassée is their favourite. This recipe results in a rather refined kind of lamb stew.

Place 900g (2lb) diced lamb in a saucepan with 3 large sliced onions, 3 or 4 spring onions, with most of the green stems being used as well, 1 or 2 lettuces, broken as for a salad, some finely chopped fresh parsley or dill, or both. Add sufficient water or stock to cover completely, salt and pepper to taste, and simmer until the meat is quite tender.

Add an Egg and Lemon Sauce (see page 165) very slowly. Stir until the sauce has had a chance to thicken. Serve hot with peas or, if you like, rice or mashed potatoes.

Generally Greeks prefer to steep lettuces in boiling water before putting them into meat dishes. It is considered that this removes their slightly bitter flavour.

Roast Lamb

Arni Psito

In every taverna, or almost every large taverna, you will see several small roasts of lamb, at first glance looking rather dried. But on tasting you will find them tender and garlic-flavoured.

1 leg lamb	*4 cloves garlic*
Juice 1 lemon	*50g (2oz) butter*
225ml (8fl oz) hot water	*Salt and pepper*

Peel the garlic and cut it into thin slivers. Wipe the meat clean and cut small incisions in it. Into these insert the garlic. Rub well with salt, pepper and lemon juice. Melt the butter, add the meat and gently roast it for 1 hour, then add the hot water and continue roasting until the meat is very tender. Baste fairly frequently. Quite often small potatoes are added during the last 45 minutes of cooking, they will become brown and soft but not crisp as the English style of roast potatoes for there is too much water in the pan. However, their taste is very good for they have absorbed much of the garlic-flavoured gravy.

Baked Lamb, Peasant Style

Arni Sto Pourno Horiatiko

900g (2lb) lamb, breast or shoulder	*2 tablespoons olive oil*
450g (1lb) feta cheese (see page 217)	*Salt and pepper to taste*
900g (2lb) peeled and sliced tomatoes	

Cut the meat into large cubes. Put these into a baking pan. Cut the cheese into smaller cubes and arrange these on top of the meat. Cover with tomatoes and sprinkle with salt and pepper. Sprinkle with oil and bake at 190°C/375°F/Gas 5 until the meat is very tender, basting carefully from time to time.

Greek cooking

Minced Lamb and Noodles

Hilopites Me Kima

No exact measurements are required for this simple dish but if you use about 900g (2lb) minced meat you should use 450g (1lb) of broken noodles.

Fry the minced lamb in olive oil or butter, flavouring it with as much finely chopped onion, crushed garlic, peeled and chopped tomatoes, salt and pepper as taste dictates. Simmer until these ingredients have the appearance of a really thick sauce. Heat a pan of water until it is boiling, add salt and the noodles. Cook rapidly for 10 minutes, drain, and if by this time the meat is tender and you have a thick sauce, stir in the drained noodles and continue cooking very slowly for another 10 minutes.

Lamb Cutlets in Paper

Arnissia Paithakia Sto Harti

Half-fry as many lamb cutlets as required, using either olive oil or butter or a mixture of both. Remove the cutlets from the pan and keep hot. Into the same fat put some chopped onion, tomato paste or purée, salt, pepper, chopped fresh parsley to taste and enough dry white wine to bring this to a sauce consistency. Simmer until the sauce is reduced and quite thick. Place each cutlet on a separate piece of oiled greaseproof paper, and pour one tablespoon of sauce over each. Wrap the cutlets, arrange in a baking tin, each package close to the other, and bake at 190°C/375°F/Gas 5 for about 30 to 40 minutes, the time depending largely on the size and quality of the cutlets. As long as the oven is not too hot, long cooking will do the cutlets no harm, for they are well protected.

Lamb Cutlets in Marjoram Sauce

Arnissia Paithakia Riyanata

Allow 2 or 3 (or more) cutlets per person; rub them with salt, pepper and lemon juice and arrange them in a shallow fireproof casserole. Brown them quickly in butter, cover with the marjoram sauce and bake at 190°C/375°F/Gas 5 (or cook on top of the stove) until tender.

Sauce. Mix in a basin 3 tablespoons of olive oil, salt, pepper and 1 heaped teaspoon of dried marjoram. Add the juice of 2 large lemons and 125ml (4fl oz) of stock or water. Stir and when the mixture is blended pour it over the chops. A little dry white wine may be added.

Sauce enough for about 9 cutlets. Serve in the casserole.

Lamb Grilled on Skewers (Kebabs)

Arni Souvlakia

This is one of the simplest and best dishes of the Balkans, for no one can pretend that grilled lamb belongs to any one Balkan country, or for that matter any Arab or Asian country. I could almost write a book on kebabs. From Yugoslavia to Persia and on to Pakistan and Malaya meat is spiced, skewered and grilled over charcoal.

Cut the meat from a leg of lamb into cubes about 2.5cm (1in) square. Rub with salt, pepper, lemon juice, olive oil and marjoram. Impale the meat on skewers and grill or barbecue them over charcoal, turning the skewer from time to time to avoid burning the meat. Serve still on the skewers on a bed of fresh parsley or watercress and with thick wedges of lemon.

You will also find grilled and skewered lamb with each piece interspersed with thick wedges of tomato, or onion, or a bay leaf, it is really a matter of taste. The really long skewers look the most effective for any type of kebab.

Greek cooking

Lamb on a Spit (Turning Kebab)

Donner Kebab

This form of kebab is not made at home although in the Balkans you can always organize a cook to come and prepare these kebabs in your garden for a special occasion. The meat, always lamb, highly flavoured with garlic, herbs and spices, is cut from the rump into long strips and then wound round the spit (or skewer). This is fixed in a vertical position near a vertical charcoal fire with its opening in front instead of at the top. The spit revolves all the time the lamb is cooking, hence its name. The meat is carved off vertically in thin slices with a very sharp knife and as it is carved it drops into a small tin pan with a handle. An exact portion is carved, leaving the raw underlayer of meat now exposed to the fire and it in turn is nicely grilled. The kebab which started in the morning the shape of an enormous carrot gets smaller and smaller. In the evening, as a general rule, there is nothing left but the spit and the dying embers of the fire. But by this time it is very late indeed.

Each portion of the kebab is laid on a 'bed' of finely sliced onion, freshly chopped parsley and lightly sprinkled with red pepper.

Trayodia, Goat Song

For a great many people in this world, including gourmets, goat and sheep are interchangeable. Most British people turn pale if asked to eat goat, although many of us have eaten and enjoyed goat and kid under the impression we were eating lamb.

The Greeks, however, appreciate young goat and kid as much as they do yearling lamb and the milk-lamb. They refuse to eat 'lamb' when it has reached the age of mutton. It has, they say, a peculiar odour, and they grimace as they curl their tongues inside their mouths to show the effect this muttony flavour has on their palates. They feel as strongly about mutton as the Briton does about goat.

For the Greeks the goat has long been a symbol in mythology. When the shepherds in the mountains saw the light, gambolling mountain goat, fleet of foot, daring and apparently full of the pleasure of life, they created Pan in the image of the goat, symbolizing the joy of living.

The goat has also been the subject of songs from the ancient playwrights and poets such as Sophocles, Euripides and Aeschylus. In the theatre of

Meat
Kreata

Dionysus the dramas celebrating the God of Spring, of Corn and Wine, had actors clothed in goatskins who danced a chorus to the sound of flutes and drums. One day a man named Thespis suddenly broke the ranks of the chorus and started to argue with the leader of the chorus. This was the first dialogue in the theatre and Thespis the first actor who spoke on the stage. From that time on the Greeks called the spoken stageshow 'Trayodia', which means goatsong. And the goat was also an animal considered fit for sacrifice to the great gods of Greek mythology.

There is a charming story told of Noah and his animals after the Flood when his ark had come to rest. According to this it was the goat which led Noah to the discovery of wine. Noah, it was said, loved the goats best of all the animals in his ark and would watch over them most carefully. One day he noticed that one of the billy goats did not stay with the other animals once the ark was on dry land but went his own mysterious way. Noah watched him and discovered that the goat in the evening would go skipping and jumping down the hill, obviously intent on something important. Noah, curious, followed the goat and saw it nibbling contentedly at a great vine 'bearing luscious and heavy fruit'. Noah also picked a bunch of grapes intending to take it back to show his family, but on his way back he absent-mindedly nibbled at the grapes. Finding them quite delicious he went back to the vine and ate some more. The goat was still with him. Noah and the goat meandered down the hill together and Noah noticed the gaily prancing goat was uncertain on his legs; Noah too found his legs were heavy although his head felt light. He had no cares and by the time they reached the bottom of the hill he too was prancing and dancing as merrily as the goat. However, back at the door of the ark he collapsed and his unhappy children, taking him for dead, laid him out on his bed and wept. But the next morning the old patriarch awoke hale and hearty and told the story of the vine. He took his family along to try the grapes as well. Since that day man has known the pleasures of wine and owes it all to the billy goat. Not the biblical version.

Muslims also eat goat and the Prophet Mohammed pronounced: 'There is no house possessing a goat but that blessing abideth therein.' Solomon of the Jews sang: 'Thy hair is as a flock of goats.' So the goat has a history of its own, and one of which it can be proud.

The Italian peasants eat kid or young goat at Easter; the Mexicans, the Californians, even the Texans, eat kid and goat. It is as at home in the modern world as it was in the ancient. The goat can thrive on almost nothing. The rocky and barren Greek and Middle Eastern soil where there

continued

Greek cooking

are waterless hills and only the grey asphodel grows, is the home of the nimble goat. A goat will climb to heights that sheep or other domestic animals would fear; his is a free spirit, and he will venture far. He is as much at home in the towns as in the country, in the Eastern world as in the Western. In the high mountain ranges of India goats mean more to goatherds than do their wives, and perhaps this is to be understood, for the goat has long hair which can be used in making valuable wool for blankets, and the mountain goat has no objection to being used as a pack animal.

Goat's milk has more vitamin B and albumen than cow's milk, while butter made from it, although white, has a higher proportion of vitamin A than cow's milk butter. In goat's milk too there is a softer curd and less fat. The Greeks have been drinking goat's milk since before there was an England. Aristotle wrote that the milk of the goat is the best of all milk and most easily acceptable to the stomach of man.

Because Greeks like kid they breed their goats to have their kids in the spring and when they are ready for eating they have a feast. Here then is the Greek recipe for dealing with kid, a recipe that can be used for lamb or even mutton.

Roast Kid

Katsikaki Psito

Rub a whole kid with lemon juice, salt and pepper, and insert slivers of garlic into its skin; score it lightly. Arrange it in a baking pan and quickly sear in a hot oven, then add olive oil or butter, some mountain herbs, if available, otherwise herbs of your own choice such as parsley or a bouquet garni, and roast the meat at 190°C/375°F/Gas 5 until it is almost tender. Add 225ml (8fl oz) of water to the pan, baste with this frequently and continue roasting until the meat is very tender, almost dropping off the bones. Serve with peas and tomatoes, if you like, even with mint sauce or cranberry jelly.

Sometimes the kid is served with a spiced and fragrant wine sauce. This is simply made by adding red wine to the gravy, bringing it once to the boil and straining it. This addition, however, is an Italian influence.

Braised Veal

Moscari Kapama

This is an extremely popular dish despite the Greek preference for lamb. Quantities vary according to taste and there is no exact recipe.

Brown 1.4kg (3lb) diced veal in butter or oil in a baking tin, but on top of the stove. Add a fair amount of chopped onion and also some chopped garlic. Let this brown, then stir 25g (1oz) of plain flour into the pan, add dry red wine to cover, salt, pepper, and cinnamon to taste. Gently simmer, until the meat is tender. Slow, very slow, simmering gives the veal something of the flavour of game. Chopped and peeled tomatoes may be added, as well as chopped fresh parsley and other herbs.

Can be served with fried or mashed potatoes, or any of the pastas, or cauliflower, it really does not matter which.

Veal with Macaroni, Corfu Style

Pastitsada Kerkireïkïa

Chop very finely a good quantity of onions. Heat enough oil to fry the onions until they begin to change colour. Brown as much diced veal as required lightly with the onions. Add either a large quantity of peeled and chopped tomatoes or some thick Tomato Sauce and enough water and dry white wine to cover. Add salt, pepper and herbs to taste. Remember that the veal is to be eaten with either macaroni or spaghetti so that plenty of sauce is required.

Cook the macaroni (or spaghetti) in the usual manner, drain and stir into it some melted butter. Take most of the sauce from the pan and stir this into the macaroni. Serve with the meat on a platter.

Garlic may be added to taste.

Greek cooking

Veal Ragout

Moscari Ragout

900g (2lb) diced veal
900g (2lb) small onions
Chopped garlic to taste
1 bay leaf
150ml (1/4 pint) dry red wine

75g (3oz) butter
Salt and pepper
Egg and Lemon Sauce
(see page 165)

Melt the butter in a saucepan, brown the meat, add the onions and when these are brown, but only just, add the wine, garlic, salt, pepper, bay leaf and enough water to cover. Cover and simmer until the gravy is thick and the meat quite tender. If more liquid is required it can be added, either more red wine but not too much, or more hot water, or a mixture of both. Add the Egg and Lemon Sauce 5 minutes before serving.

An exceedingly good winter dish which goes well with boiled rice or creamed potatoes.

Minced Veal with Noodles

Macaroni Me Kreas (Youvetsi)

450g (1lb) cooked noodles
  or tagliatelle
450g (1lb) minced veal
50–75g (2–3oz) butter
150ml (1/4 pint) dry red wine
3 finely chopped onions

150ml (1/4 pint) Tomato Sauce
  (see pages 169–170)
1 tablespoon finely chopped
  fresh parsley
Salt and pepper

Put the meat into a pan with a little water and cook until the liquid is absorbed. Add the butter, onions, parsley, wine and seasoning and cook very slowly until the meat and the onions are tender. Put half the noodles into a baking dish, cover with all the meat and onion mixture, add the remaining noodles and the Tomato Sauce and bake at 190°C/375°F/Gas 5 for about 20 minutes.

Veal Ragout *(Dodecanese Style)*

Moscari Stifatho

900g (2lb) veal
20 small onions
2 cloves chopped garlic
125ml (4fl oz) dry white wine
 or wine vinegar

4–6 large, peeled and coarsely
 chopped tomatoes
1 bay leaf
50–75g (2–3oz) butter
Salt and pepper

Melt the butter and brown the meat. Transfer the meat from the pan to a saucepan and brown the onions and garlic in the same fat. Add 600ml (1 pint) of water, wine and tomatoes and stir all this together, season generously and pour this mixture over the meat. Stir, cover the pan and cook over a very slow heat for at least 2 hours; if you can, simmer it for even longer. The pot should remain covered all the time. If you feel that perhaps the meat is sticking to the bottom of the pan, shake it from time to time, but if the heat is really low there should be no danger of either burning or sticking. This type of stew is extremely rich and for those who enjoy onions very palatable indeed. Enough for 4 or 5 people.

Pork with Celery and Egg and Lemon Sauce

Hirino Me Selinorizes

An excellent dish and the speciality of more than one of the Athenian tavernas.

If using ordinary white celery, use a large head and all of the stalks plus as much as possible of the leaves. If celeriac, peel it first and cut into cubes. About 450g (1lb) of the latter should be sufficient.

900g–1.4kg (2–3lb) diced pork
50–75g (2–3oz) butter
2 medium chopped onions
Handful chopped fresh parsley

25g (1oz) plain flour
Salt and pepper
Egg and Lemon Sauce
 (see page 165)

continued

Greek cooking

150ml (1/4 pint) dry red or white wine
450g (1lb) celeriac or 1 large head
  and leaves of celery

Melt the butter and quickly brown the meat, add the onions and, as they begin to brown, stir in the flour, blend, then add the wine and the parsley. Pour in enough hot water to cover, add salt and pepper, and simmer over a slow heat for at least 2 hours.

If you are using celeriac, it must be put with the meat about 30 minutes after it has been simmering, or even with the wine and parsley. Celeriac is a root vegetable and requires long cooking. Ordinary celery can be added to the meat about 45 minutes before it is ready.

Add the Egg and Lemon Sauce just before serving, stir it well into the liquid, simmer for 5 minutes, then stand on the side of the stove, covered, for 5 minutes more.

Pork Chops in Red Wine

Hirines Brizoles Krassates

This seems to me almost straight Italian but the Greeks shrug their expressive shoulders and say, 'Well, maybe, but we eat it regularly all the same.'

Trim and simmer in boiling water as many pork chops as required. When they are partially cooked, drain off the water and add enough butter or other fat to brown the meat. When browned on both sides, add dry red wine to cover and simmer gently until the meat is quite tender.

The chops will have a far nicer flavour if they are rubbed with salt, pepper and lemon juice 30 minutes before using.

Beef cooked with Vegetables

Vothinó Me Lahaniká

900g (2lb) braising steak
50g (2oz) butter
12 small onions
3 sliced carrots

4 sliced potatoes
2–3 chopped stalks celery
2 coarsely chopped leeks
Salt and pepper

This is a simple but most appetizing dish. Cut the beef into pieces the size of a walnut and brown them in butter. Add the onions, carrots, potatoes, celery and leeks, from the last two ingredients use as much of the green as possible. Cover with water, add salt and pepper, and cook until the meat and vegetables are tender. At this point you can remove the meat and rub the vegetables through a sieve and then return the purée to the meat, or you can serve the meat with the vegetables left as they are. Chopped garlic may also be added.

Beef Stew

Vothinó Stifatho

1.4kg (3lb) stewing steak
1.4kg (3lb) small onions
1 large onion finely chopped
75g (3oz) butter
2 tablespoons vinegar
150ml (1/4 pint) dry white wine

1 large clove chopped garlic
150ml (1/4 pint) fresh tomato juice
1 bay leaf
Salt and pepper to taste
600ml (1 pint) hot water

Cut the meat into stew-sized pieces. Heat 50g (2oz) of butter and lightly brown the chopped onion and the meat. Add tomato juice, vinegar, wine, about half the hot water, bay leaf, garlic, salt and pepper and cook over a medium heat until the meat is tender. In the meantime peel the small onions and brown these separately in another pan with the remaining butter. Add them to the beef and at the same time pour in the remaining hot water, or enough to cover. Continue to cook slowly until the small onions are soft.

Some Greeks remove the onions before serving the stew but this is not usual.

Greek cooking

Beef Loaf

Rouló

900g (2lb) minced beef
225ml (8fl oz) soft breadcrumbs
2–3 hard-boiled eggs
1 large minced onion
2 tablespoons finely chopped
  fresh parsley

1 beaten raw egg
225ml (8fl oz) dry red wine
225ml (8fl oz) tomato juice
Salt and pepper
75g (3oz) butter

Mix the beef, breadcrumbs, onion, parsley, salt and pepper and knead to a paste. Spread out on to a chopping board. Put the hard-boiled eggs in the centre, then roll up the meat. Brush with beaten egg. Melt the butter in a heavy based frying pan and carefully lift the meat roll into the pan. Fry to a golden brown, first on one side, then on the other. Add the wine, cover the pan and simmer for a few minutes; add the tomato juice, just a little water, and continue to cook slowly for about 45 minutes.

Rouló is usually served surrounded with noodles, but peas, potatoes or other vegetables may be used instead.

Cut the loaf into thick slices, arrange down the centre of a hot platter and pour the sauce over the meat and noodles, or vegetables.

Rolled Beef with Noodles

Rouló Me Makarónia

A Macedonian dish but available in most Greek towns.

1.4kg (3lb) rolled sirloin steak	1 bay leaf
1 clove chopped garlic	Salt and pepper
300ml (½ pint) thick tomato juice	600ml (1 pint) boiling water
75g (3oz) butter	or stock

Rub the meat with salt and pepper. Insert the garlic into the meat. Melt the butter in a baking pan and brown the meat, then bake at 190°C/375°F/Gas 5 until tender. Add the liquid and leave the meat in the oven until this reboils. Take the rolled meat from the pan and thickly slice it. Put the pan on the top of the stove, add the bay leaf and tomato juice. Stir this well into the gravy, return the meat to the pan and continue to cook slowly until the sauce thickens.

Noodles. These are cooked separately and for this particular dish square noodles are recommended. The quantity depends on appetites, but, however much you cook, the noodles should be boiled in plenty of boiling, salted water until tender. Drain and stir into the noodles a generous lump of butter. Serve with the meat on the same platter.

Greek cooking

Marjoram Beef Steaks

Vothinó Filléto Riyanáto

Medium-thick sirloin steaks
Lemon juice
Marjoram

Butter
Salt and pepper

Arrange the steaks on a grill pan. Spread lightly with butter, sprinkle generously with lemon juice, add salt and pepper, and flavour to taste with marjoram, either fresh or dried. Grill the meat until brown on one side, turn it over and repeat the process. Baste with the juice which falls from the meat and serve the steaks as hot as possible, lightly sprinkled with lemon juice and garnished with a knob of butter flavoured with marjoram.

Steak in a Garlic Sauce

Sofrito

This is a recipe from the island of Corfu where the cooking is much influenced by both the Italians and the British. The steak used in this recipe need not be of the finest quality, although obviously if you want to prepare a really tender steak in this manner there is nothing to prevent you. Living most of my life in what some people call 'foreign parts', I have become used to steaks of dubious origins and I find this recipe covers a multitude of sins.

The recipe I have comes from the owner of the Corfu Restaurant in Athens, which serves Corfu specialities. The proprietor declared that all his produce was flown in by plane from Corfu to Athens, including fish. As we talked the restaurant was beginning to fill up with hungry mainland Greeks and others, but each waiter, as he passed the table where I was busy learning about Corfu cooking from the proprietor, would throw in his contribution and his special bit of knowledge. Afterwards I was taken into the kitchen where a practical demonstration was given. Later, much later, that evening I returned to the restaurant to eat *sofrito*, and enjoy it. Now we eat it often, utilizing our dubious steaks.

Cut as much rump steak as required into fairly large pieces, beat it for a while and make slits all over the surface of the flesh, this is to prevent shrinking. Remove all sinews. Rub with salt and pepper and coat it quite thickly with plain flour. Melt butter (yes, it was insisted, butter, not olive oil) and fry the pieces of meat until browned. Sprinkle with plain flour. Now add a really generous quantity of finely chopped garlic (a whole head if you like and can take it), plenty of salt and pepper, and when the garlic begins to change colour add enough dry red wine mixed with a little vinegar to make a thick sauce. Put all this into a casserole, add some water and bring to the boil. Reduce the heat and continue cooking slowly until the meat is really tender and the sauce thick. Serve with creamed potatoes and as hot as possible.

As you will see, this is a recipe which can be made to requirements and for which one does not need exact measurements. The main point is that the sauce should be thick and taste of garlic.

Greek cooking

Beef and Mixed Vegetable Casserole

Kreas Ke Lahanika Sti Catsarola

This recipe comes from a Macedonian Greek friend and has much of the Bosnian flavour.

900g (2lb) diced braising steak
1 small white cabbage
4–5 large potatoes
4 large tomatoes
2 large green peppers, seeded

3 large onions
1 small red cabbage
225g (8oz) dried butter beans
1 bottle dry white wine
Salt and black pepper

Cut the beef into slices. Soak the beans overnight and cook next day until almost soft. Peel and slice the potatoes and tomatoes, cut the white and red cabbage into strips and mix. The onions can be sliced or chopped according to taste.

At the bottom of a casserole arrange one layer of meat, then add a layer of all the vegetables in turn. Continue in this way until all the ingredients are used up, the top layer should be either of tomatoes or potatoes. Sprinkle each layer generously with salt and pepper. Add the white wine, cover and gently simmer for at least 3 hours. The result is a thoroughly delicious dish, rich and aromatic. You can also add a layer of peeled and sliced aubergine and marrow, even peas and carrots, it really does not matter.

Serve in the casserole in which it is cooked.

Meat and Potato Pie

Mousakas I

450g (1lb) minced beef or lamb
900g (2lb) peeled and
  sliced potatoes
2 large sliced onions
Handful finely chopped
fresh parsley

50g (2oz) butter
3–4 peeled and sliced tomatoes
50g (2oz) grated Cheddar cheese
Salt and pepper
300ml (1/2 pint) Béchamel Sauce
  (see page 165)

Put the meat, onions and parsley into a pan with a little water and simmer until all the water is absorbed. Add the butter and cook slowly for about 20 minutes, then add the tomatoes, salt and pepper. Continue to cook for another 15 minutes or until the tomatoes are soft. Grease a round casserole and arrange a layer of potatoes at the bottom, overlapping the slices, then add a layer of the meat and tomato mixture, another of potatoes and continue until these ingredients are finished. The top layer should be of potatoes. Add the Cheddar cheese to the sauce and pour this over the potatoes. Bake at 190°C/375°F/Gas 5 for about 1 hour.

Some Greeks prefer to fry the potatoes very lightly first.

Mousaka, Salonica Style

Mousakas II

8 medium-sized aubergines
700g (1½lb) minced beef or lamb
3 minced onions
Handful finely chopped fresh parsley
100g (4oz) breadcrumbs
1–2 tablespoons tomato juice
Salt and pepper

Olive oil for frying
600ml (1 pint) Béchamel Sauce
  (see page 165)
2 egg yolks
Grated Cheddar cheese
Butter

First peel and slice the aubergines, sprinkle with salt and leave between two large plates until all the water is drained from them. Wipe dry. Heat plenty of olive oil in a deep pan and fry the aubergine slices until brown on both sides. Put these on a large platter to drain.

Pour off almost all of the oil from the pan and lightly fry the minced meat and the onions until brown, then add the parsley, tomato juice, salt and pepper. Simmer for about 30 minutes then add the breadcrumbs and stir everything in the pan together.

Grease a large, square baking tin with oil and cover the bottom with fried aubergine. Spread this with half the meat and onion mixture; add another layer of aubergine and spread this with the remaining meat and onion.

Beat the egg yolks into the Béchamel Sauce and pour this over the meat. Sprinkle generously with breadcrumbs and grated Cheddar cheese, add a few slivers of butter and bake at 190°C/375°F/Gas 5 for 30 minutes. The top should be brown and like a crust. Serve hot. The correct shape for this type of mousaka is either square or oblong and the texture should be firm enough to cut it like a cake.

Meat and Aubergine Pie
(Greek-American style)

Mousakas III

4 large aubergines
700g (1 1/2lb) minced beef or lamb
3 large coarsely chopped onions
6 medium-sized tomatoes or
  1 large tin tomatoes
75g (3oz) butter
Handful finely chopped fresh parsley
2–3 beaten eggs

75g (3oz) grated Cheddar cheese
125ml (4fl oz) dry red wine
Salt and pepper to taste
450ml (3/4 pint) Béchamel Sauce
  (see page 164)
Oil for deep-frying
225g (8oz) very fine breadcrumbs

Peel and thickly slice the aubergines, sprinkle with salt and place between two large plates. Melt 50g (2oz) of the butter, add and brown the meat, then add the onions and brown these. Add the tomatoes, wine, parsley, salt and pepper and simmer until the liquid is absorbed. Cool, add the eggs, Cheddar cheese and half the breadcrumbs.

Heat plenty of oil in a deep pan, wipe the slices of aubergine and brown each piece on both sides. Sprinkle the bottom of a casserole with the remaining breadcrumbs, cover with a layer of fried aubergine, cover this with a layer of the meat mixture, another of aubergine, then of meat and continue until all the ingredients are used up, finishing with aubergine. Cover thickly with the Béchamel Sauce and bake at 190°C/375°F/Gas 5 for about 1 hour.

This mousaka is rich but it can be made less so by not frying the aubergine before putting it into the casserole. If this is done, bake more slowly and for 30 minutes longer.

Greek cooking

Minced Meat Casserole (Rhodes)

Sfogato

700g (1½lb) minced beef or lamb
450g (1lb) courgettes, peeled
 and cubed
4 eggs
Handful chopped fresh parsley

2 large minced onions
Salt and pepper
300ml (½ pint) stock or water
50–75g (2–3oz) butter

Melt the butter, add the onions and when they change colour add the meat.
Add the courgettes, liquid, salt, pepper and parsley and cook over a low
heat until the meat is tender and the sauce fairly thick.

Beat the eggs until light and quite fluffy; let the meat mixture cool slightly,
then fold the beaten eggs into it. Pour into a casserole and bake at
190°C/375°F/Gas 5 until firm.

Failing courgettes use a small vegetable marrow. If you put the casserole
into a pan with boiling water (and in the oven) the eggs will cook more
slowly and set better.

This is an excellent way of dealing with not-so-tender meat. Serve with a
Tomato Sauce and green vegetables or salad.

Sfogato is a kind of meat and vegetable custard.

Cephalonian Pie

Kreatopita

The chief feature in the preparation of this pie is that it is made with three kinds of meat, usually lamb, goat or kid, and chicken. As goat is not widely available, use beef or pork instead.

Filling

1.8kg (4lb) mixed meats, coarsely minced
350g (12oz) chopped onions
225g (8oz) butter
450g (1lb) peeled, chopped tomatoes
100g (4oz) long-grain rice
100g (4oz) grated Kasseri cheese or Parmesan
1–2 bay leaves
Pinch salt

Pinch sugar
Handful chopped fresh parsley (optional)
1 teaspoon sugar
25g (1oz) stoned raisins (or sultanas)
6 well-beaten eggs
300ml (1/2 pint) dry white wine
8 finely chopped cloves garlic
Salt and pepper to taste

Short crust

575g (1¼lb) sifted plain flour
350g (12oz) butter
2 eggs

Warm water or milk for mixing
Ground cinnamon
Olive oil

Cook the onions in water until they are soft, then drain. Heat the butter and fry the onions until they begin to change colour. Add the white wine, the tomatoes, rice, meat, raisins, salt, pepper, garlic, sugar and bay leaves and simmer gently for about 20 minutes or until the meat is tender. Add the grated cheese and the eggs. Stir as you add the eggs to prevent them from curdling. When the ingredients are all blended remove the pan from the heat and leave until cooled.

Make the pie crust. Put the flour into a large bowl, add sugar and salt and then add the butter, rubbing it in with the fingers until the mixture becomes crumbly. Add the eggs and gradually the warm milk or water. Knead for 10 minutes until the dough is very soft, and then chill.

Divide the dough into two portions, one slightly larger than the other, and

continued

roll these out on a floured board. The bottom layer should be fairly thick and large enough to line a baking pan. Fill this with the filling, spreading it evenly, and cover with the remaining pastry. Brush this lightly with olive oil, score the top and crimp the edges slightly. Prick with a fork and sprinkle with ground cinnamon. Bake at 190°C/375°F/Gas 5 for about 1 hour or until the surface is lightly browned. If it becomes brown too quickly place a wet sheet of paper on the top until the pie is baked. Let it 'settle' for a few minutes after taking it from the oven and then cut into squares to serve.

This is a popular Carnival and Ascension Day dish with the inhabitants of the Island of Cephos. It is very rich. This recipe makes a really large pie, for at least 10 to 12 persons, and could be served as a party piece. The meats can be varied. Try mutton, lamb and veal mixed, or pork, chicken and veal, it really does not matter. As it is a dry pie, with no gravy at all, it is ideal for a buffet party.

Meat with Quinces

Kreas Me Kythonia

1.4kg (3lb) meat (lamb, veal or beef)
1.8kg (4lb) quinces
1–2 onions
50–75g (2–3oz) butter

Salt and pepper
1 teaspoon sugar
600ml (1 pint) hot water

Finely chop the onion. Peel the quinces and cut into thick slices. Heat the butter and fry the onion and the meat until brown. Add the hot water and cook slowly until the meat is tender. Add the quinces, a little more water if required, salt, pepper and sugar and cook until soft.

No other vegetables are required.

Minced Meat with Béchamel Sauce

Pastitsio

One thing is quite certain; that even the most unobservant foreigner in any part of Greece will discover that *pastitsio* is a popular and very frequent Greek dish. Sometimes it will be very good and at other times incredibly stodgy. At its best it is simply minced meat cooked slowly in a shallow pan with macaroni and covered with Béchamel Sauce (see page 165) and usually generously sprinkled with grated cheese. Sometimes bits of chopped ham are included which, although it adds quite a flavour, is deplored by the more traditionally minded. When it is stodgy it is a mixture of solid noodles and very little meat.

Meat with Chestnuts

Kreas Me Kastana

900g (2lb) fresh chestnuts
1.8kg (4lb) diced veal or beef
1–2 onions

50–75g (2–3oz) butter
Salt and pepper

Finely chop the onions. Boil the chestnuts until it is easy to peel off the brown skins.

Melt the butter and fry the onions until just brown, then add the meat. When this is brown, add 600ml (1 pint) of water, salt and pepper and cook slowly until the meat is tender. Add the chestnuts and continue to cook slowly until the chestnuts are soft.

In many Greek homes chestnuts and potatoes are interchangeable.

Greek cooking

Greek Rissoles

Keftethes

This type of small rissole or meat ball is popular throughout the Balkans, the Middle and Far East. The Greeks serve them on almost all of their festive occasions, for weddings, christenings, picnics, etc.

700g (1½lb) minced lamb or pork
100g (4oz) soft breadcrumbs
  (moistened in milk)
3 small minced onions
2 well-beaten eggs
Handful chopped fresh parsley
1 teaspoon chopped fresh mint

1 tablespoon grated Cheddar
  cheese
Salt and pepper
Plain flour
Olive oil or butter for frying
Enough ouzo to moisten
  (see pages 236–7)

The ouzo is optional and is not used by all Greek cooks. It adds just a little something unusual in flavour to the meat balls.

Put the minced onions into a strainer and pour boiling water over them. Squeeze the breadcrumbs. Mix the meat, onions, parsley, salt, pepper, breadcrumbs, mint, ouzo, cheese and eggs to a paste and leave for 30 minutes. Shape into balls, dust lightly in flour and fry in hot oil or butter until brown. Serve hot.

These meatballs should not be large, about the size of a walnut. If you are not going to use ouzo, add instead some lemon juice, about 2 tablespoons is enough of either.

An Australian-Greek told me her mother covers her *keftethes* with lemon leaves for a while if they are going to eat them cold but warned me they must not be left too long covered otherwise they will become very bitter.

Meat Balls in Egg and Lemon Sauce

Youvarlakia

900g (2lb) minced lamb, veal or beef
1 large finely chopped onion
3 tablespoons uncooked long-grain rice
2 tablespoons chopped fresh parsley
Salt and pepper

75g (3oz) butter
1 egg white slightly beaten
Egg and Lemon Sauce
  (see page 165)

Mix together the meat, parsley, rice, onion, egg white, salt and pepper and knead to a smooth paste. Break off pieces the size of a walnut, roll lightly into balls and leave for 1 hour.

Put 1.2 litres (2 pints) of water and the butter into a saucepan, bring it to the boil, add the meat balls carefully to avoid breaking them and simmer over a low heat for 30 minutes. Take the pan from the stove.

Take some of the liquid and mix with the Egg and Lemon Sauce, and pour this over the meat balls. Return the pan to the stove and cook the meat balls in the sauce over a very low heat until the sauce just begins to thicken. Serve the meat balls with the sauce.

Youvarlakia are usually served without any addition, even of potatoes. Instead of water, strained meat stock may be used, in which case use less butter.

Greek cooking

Meat with Green Olives

Kreas Me Elies

For this recipe olives in brine are required.

1.4kg (3lb) minced steak
450g (1lb) green olives
1.2 litres (2 pints) Tomato Sauce
  (see pages 169–170)

100g (4oz) butter
1 teaspoon sugar
Pepper

First deal with the olives. Carefully remove the stones, then drop them all into boiling water. Leave for 30 minutes. Wash 2 or 3 times in cold water.

Melt the butter and brown the slices of meat on both sides. Add the Tomato Sauce, plenty of pepper, sugar and the olives. Simmer gently until the meat is tender. You may require salt but not much since the brine from the olives will be salty enough.

This is a speciality in one of the many Greek monasteries.

Smyrna Sausages or Meat Balls I

Soudzoukakia I

Sausages

900g (2lb) minced veal or pork
Handful finely chopped fresh parsley
2 cloves chopped garlic
2 slices white bread
150ml (1/4 pint) dry red wine
2 beaten eggs

Olive oil for frying, or butter
150ml (1/4 pint) dry vermouth
  (optional)
Plain flour
Salt and pepper

Soak the bread in the wine until the latter is completely absorbed. Mix the meat with the parsley, garlic, salt, pepper and bread, and knead to a paste. Bind with the eggs and leave for 30 minutes. Make the Tomato Sauce. Shape the meat into small fat sausages and lightly roll in flour. Heat either oil or butter and fry the sausages until brown. Pour the vermouth into the pan and let this entirely evaporate. Add the Tomato Sauce and continue cooking for about 15 minutes, do not stir but shake the pan from time to time to avoid sticking. Serve with rice or mashed potatoes.

Tomato Sauce

50g (2oz) tomato purée
600ml (1 pint) water
50g (2oz) butter

Salt and pepper
1 teaspoon sugar

Heat the butter, add the tomato purée diluted with some of the water, stir until blended, then add sugar, salt, pepper and the remaining water. Simmer for 15 minutes until the sauce begins to thicken.

Greek cooking

Smyrna Sausages or Meat Balls II

Soudzoukakia II

700g (1 1/2lb) minced lamb or pork
100g (4oz) soft breadcrumbs
150ml (1/4 pint) dry red wine
300ml (1/2 pint) tomato juice or sauce

Salt and pepper
Pinch cumin (see page 228)
Butter for frying

Stir the crumbs and the wine together until the crumbs are moistened. Combine with the meat, salt, pepper and cumin until smooth. Shape into sausages and leave for 30 minutes. Heat about 50g (2oz) of butter and fry the rissoles until brown, then add the tomato juice and simmer gently until the meat is quite cooked, about 30 minutes. Serve with rice or potatoes, or with a green salad.

Liver in a Sauce

Sikotakia Me Saltsa

A recipe from Rhodes, a charming island which has taken some of its cooking as well as its wine from the Italians.

Marinate about 225g (8oz) of chopped calves' liver in dry red wine for an hour or more. Heat about 4 tablespoons of olive oil in a pan and lightly brown 2 small sliced onions. Take the liver from the wine, pat it dry and lightly coat in well-seasoned flour. Brown the liver, you may have to add a little more oil if the onions have absorbed too much, stir in a little marjoram or rosemary, the red wine in which you marinated the liver, and cook slowly until the sauce has thickened and the liver is tender. Serve hot with creamed potatoes.

I first ate liver cooked in this way on the wide seafront of the main town of Rhodes and asked the proprietor for the recipe. I rather wondered at the time whether the liver had really been marinated in wine as the cook had told me, but I discovered later that wine is very cheap, cheaper probably than vinegar, and certainly the sauce had the flavour of wine.

Kidneys can be cooked in exactly the same way.

Greek cooking

Poultry and Game
Poulerika ke Kyniyi

In all the following recipes I am assuming that the cook knows how to clean and prepare a fowl or game bird for cooking. Usually those sufficiently interested in cooking to buy books giving international recipes also have on their bookshelves those equally important basic cooking books which give accurate and graphic descriptions for the more complicated operations needed with birds. So I assume, when explaining the following recipes for cooking feathered creatures in the Greek manner, that they are already cleaned and prepared for pots of various kinds.

There is one tip I would like to pass on, although it is not strictly Greek but came from the French wife of a Greek friend. When her chickens are ready for cooking, whether she is going to steam, boil, roast or fry them, she puts them in the kitchen sink and pours over them a kettle of boiling water. This causes them to plump out and whiten and it makes it easier for any type of cooking. She also insisted that the flavour is much improved by this method of hers, but there I am not sure. Other improvements I can vouch for and, in fact, I have always acted on her advice since.

As far as chickens are concerned, only young and plump birds should be used for roasting, frying, steaming or boiling. The older, skinnier ones are best left for soup making or, at the very most, used minced.

In the matter of game, the Greeks do not hang their birds as long as we do. So whether the following game recipes are made with birds which have been hung or with fresh ones, depends entirely on the taste of the individual cook. Rabbits can also be given the boiled kettle treatment and are most certainly improved by being rubbed with lemon.

Cold Steamed Chicken

Kotopoulo

This is more a tip than a recipe. Steam (or boil) a chicken in any manner you prefer. When it is cold rub it thoroughly with cut lemon and leave it for at least 30 minutes before serving. This adds to the flavour and makes the flesh whiter.

Grilled Chicken and Sauce

Kotopoulo Tis Skaras Me Salsa

2 grilling chickens about 900g
  (2lb) each
Salt and pepper

Juice ½ lemon
Olive oil or butter
Garlic

Sauce

1 tablespoon olive oil
1 tablespoon lemon juice
½ teaspoon dry English mustard

1 teaspoon chopped fresh or
  dried thyme
Salt and pepper to taste

Split the chickens down the centre and rub each piece with salt, pepper and 1 cut clove of garlic, then finally with a little oil or butter. Place in a shallow pan, not too near the grill, turn from time to time and baste frequently with the sauce until they are nicely browned and tender.

To make the sauce, mix the oil and lemon until well-blended, then add salt, pepper, dry English mustard and thyme. Cook for about 3 minutes, stirring all the while.

Greek cooking

Roast Chicken with Marjoram

Kotopoulo Riyanato

1 large roasting chicken
   about 2.3kg (5lb)
50g (2oz) melted butter
50ml (2fl oz) olive oil

Juice 1/2 lemon
Salt and pepper
450ml (3/4 pint) hot water
1/4 teaspoon marjoram

Rub the chicken well with salt, pepper and lemon juice. Leave for 1 hour. Put the olive oil, butter and water into a pan and then the chicken, lying it on its back. Sprinkle the chicken with marjoram, put the pan into the oven and roast at 190°C/375°F/Gas 5, basting the chicken frequently, until it is very tender. Lift it from time to time to prevent the skin from sticking to the pan.

Chicken Stew

Kotopoulo Kapama

1 chicken about 1.8kg (4lb)
6 peeled and chopped tomatoes
2 tablespoons tomato purée
1/2 teaspoon ground cinnamon
90ml (3fl oz) olive oil

75g (3oz) butter
Juice 1 lemon
Salt and pepper
600ml (1 pint) hot water
Ground cloves

Thoroughly clean and joint the chicken. Mix with the lemon juice, the cloves, cinnamon, salt and pepper and rub each piece of the chicken well with this mixture. Heat the butter and oil together and brown the pieces of chicken, take them from the pan and keep hot. Add the tomatoes and purée, stir this well into the hot butter and oil mixture, then add the water. Cook over a gentle heat until the tomatoes are very soft, like a sauce, then return the chicken to the pan. See that each piece is well-coated with the Tomato Sauce, cover and continue to cook until the chicken meat is so tender that it almost falls off the bone.

Chicken on the Spit

Kotopoulo Tis Skaras

One of the best of Athenian dishes. This recipe is adapted for the barbecue.

Wash the chickens, they should be very young and plump, and dry them inside and out. Rub them well with salt, pepper, garlic and lemon and leave for 1 hour before grilling. Push each chicken on to a revolving spit, turn it frequently until it browns and is cooked through. If you are in doubt about its being cooked, twist the leg of one of the chickens. If it breaks easily then the chicken is ready. Delicious when served with a garlic sauce (see pages 166–7) and, when in season, watercress.

The heat, whether charcoal or electricity, must be very low, otherwise the chickens are burned on the outside and not sufficiently cooked inside.

Chicken in the Pot

Kotopoulo Sto Stamni

This is a speciality of one or two of the tavernas just outside Athens, and elsewhere in Greece.

There are no specific directions. A tender chicken, first having been rubbed with lemon juice, is gently squeezed into an earthenware pot, and wine, tomato juice, herbs, salt, pepper and some butter is added. The pot is then firmly sealed and shaken so that all the ingredients are properly mixed. It is then baked in a slow oven and the pot brought to the table for serving. The waiter, with considerable skill born of long practice, breaks the pot in front of you and the whole steaming, aromatic contents are poured out. A splendid dish.

Other meats are sometimes prepared in the same manner.

Greek cooking

Chicken with Noodles

Kotopoulo Hilopites

This chicken dish comes from the Peloponnese.

1–2 young chickens, about
  1.4kg (3lb) each
75g (3oz) butter
2 medium, finely chopped onions
225ml (8fl oz) dry white wine
1–2 cloves chopped garlic
6 peeled and chopped tomatoes
300ml (½ pint) pint thick Tomato
  Sauce (see pages 169–170),
  or soup

3–4 stalks chopped celery
2–3 tablespoons finely chopped
  fresh parsley
Pinch ground cinnamon
450g (1lb) noodles
Salt and pepper
Freshly grated cheese
  (see below)
Hot water

The Greeks use a grating cheese called *kasseri*, or sometimes they use *kefalotyri*. If neither is available, Parmesan can be substituted.

Clean the chickens and joint them into serving pieces. Rub generously with pepper and salt. Heat the butter in a thick-bottomed pan and brown the chicken pieces. Take them from the pan and keep hot. Put the onions and garlic in the same fat and when they begin to change colour, return the chicken, add the wine and simmer for 15 minutes. Add the tomatoes and the sauce, then the celery, parsley, salt and pepper and enough hot water to cover. Simmer, tightly covered, until the chicken is quite tender. About 20 minutes before the chicken is ready, start to cook the noodles in another pan in rapidly boiling, salt water. About 15 minutes before it is ready add the cinnamon to the chicken, if you put the cinnamon in too soon it will lose its flavour. Drain the noodles when tender. Take the pieces of chicken from the pan and keep hot. Add the sauce and the cheese to the noodles alternately. Arrange the noodles and the chicken on a large platter and serve hot. You can use a little more grated cheese if required as a garnish.

Chicken Pie

Kotopita

This is a pie for a party or those with a large family, made with filo pastry. Failing filo pastry the pie can be made with flaky pastry in the usual way, using, however, the Greek type of filling.

2 chickens, about 900g (2lb) each
1.4kg (3lb) sliced onions
4–6 eggs
3 tablespoons grated Cheddar cheese
About 100g (4oz) butter

300ml (1/2 pint) milk
Salt and pepper
Nutmeg
18 sheets filo pastry
(see pages 177–8)

Clean the chickens and cook them in plenty of water. Remove any scum which arises on the stock before adding the onions and salt. When the meat of the chickens is so tender that it comes away easily from the carcass, take them out of the pan and put aside. Continue to cook the onions, stirring from time to time until the mixture forms a thick purée. Bone the fowls and shred the meat. If you want to use the skin, cut it finely. When the onions have become like a sauce, add the milk and the chicken meat, stirring continuously until the mixture boils. Take from the heat. Leave until cool, then add the cheese, eggs (breaking these directly into the mixture), salt, pepper and a good pinch of nutmeg. Line a baking dish with about 6 sheets of filo pastry, greasing each sheet before putting it in the dish. Add the mixture, spreading it well over the pastry, then cover with the remaining sheets, greasing each one. Brush the top sheet with butter and score this into squares so that when it is cooked it is marked out into serving pieces, but do not actually cut through the sheets of pastry. The top layers of the covering sheets should overlap so that the mixture can be enclosed. Bake for 1 hour at 190°C/375°F/Gas 5. Usually served hot.

This same mixture served between 2 layers of ordinary puff pastry is excellent and makes a very special kind of chicken pie. When I make Greek chicken pie using flaky pastry I always bake it in a fairly shallow pan because the filling is a fairly solid one, without much gravy.

Greek cooking

Chicken Livers in Madeira Sauce

Sikotakia Tis Kottas Me Saltsa

This is a recipe from Corfu, with a strong Italian influence or flavour.

18 chicken livers
6 lamb kidneys
75–100g (3–4oz) butter
300ml (1/2 pint) chicken stock
Grated onion to taste
25g (1oz) plain flour

A little chopped fresh parsley
1–2 cloves chopped garlic
Salt and pepper
150ml (1/4 pint) Madeira wine
Creamed potatoes

Remove the white centre and skin from the lambs' kidneys and cut them into pieces in size to match the chicken livers. Melt the butter in a shallow saucepan and quickly fry the liver over a fast heat for 4 minutes, shaking the pan frequently to prevent burning or browning. Sprinkle in the flour and cook over a high heat to let the flour just brown. Mix it well into the butter to form the basis of the sauce.

Heat the chicken stock and gradually stir it into the butter and flour roux, add the onion, not too much of this otherwise the liver flavour becomes lost, the garlic and parsley and cook over a low heat, stirring all the while until this mixture begins to bubble and boil. Add salt and pepper. Take the pan from the heat, remove the livers, quickly strain the sauce, return it to the pan, add the Madeira, stir it well into the thick sauce, return the livers and carefully reheat. Serve the livers and sauce with creamed potatoes.

Goose with Apple and Chestnut Stuffing

Hina Yemisti

1 goose, about 4.5kg (10lb)	2 teaspoons sugar
4 large dessert apples	Salt and pepper
450g (1lb) canned chestnuts	

Goose is usually very fatty so it should first be pricked all over with a sharp fork. Peel, core and chop the apples and simmer gently in just enough water until they are soft, but not too soft. Add sugar, salt and pepper and the chestnuts (which I hope you have shelled and skinned!). Fill the goose with this mixture, then place it on a rack in a baking pan and roast at 190°C/375°F/Gas 5 until the flesh is tender and a golden brown. As the fat accumulates, pour it off. A goose this size will take about 3½ hours to cook.

Personally, I prefer to use whole apples. I peel and core them and stuff the cavities with chopped chestnuts. Then I push the apples and the remaining chestnuts into the goose, secure the openings with a toothpick and roast it in the usual manner. The apples are sufficiently cooked and the flavour is the same.

Some Greek cooks also like to add pine nuts and some chopped fried onion, but I do not think this is at all necessary.

Greek cooking

'Hydra' Chicken
(Chicken cooked in brandy and cream)

Kotopoulo Tis Hydras

1 young chicken, about 1.8kg (4lb)	*Butter*
150ml (1/4 pint) brandy	*Lemon*
150ml (1/4 pint) double cream	*Salt and pepper*

Another recipe, which, in all honesty, I cannot categorically claim as Greek, nor for that matter as really belonging to the Island of Hydra, a charming island where artists and writers holiday, and work. It was given to me by a distinguished Greek artist whom I met when crossing from Piraeus to Hydra with some friends.

This is his special recipe, made with Greek brandy, but he agreed any other brandy could be used. The chicken is jointed according to its size and tenderness, lightly fried in butter until a golden brown (no flour, no egg, no breadcrumbs) and then the brandy is poured over it and it is simmered until the brandy is absorbed. Then the cream is poured over the chicken pieces and, when this is just hot, the chicken is served. Quite delicious, although when one considers the matter, how could such a recipe fail, providing the chicken is young and tender? If potatoes are creamed to perfection, this is all that is needed to go with it, and this simply so that you can savour the sauce longer and wipe up every single drop.

Hare in Walnut Sauce

Layos Me Saltsa Karithia

This rather unusual Greek dish is really delicious. I do not think any of the ingredients should be omitted or substituted since they all add to the general flavour.

*1 hare or rabbit, prepared and
  cut into serving pieces
Vinegar and water in equal
  proportions*

*Handful chopped celery
4 slices of lemon
A little fresh marjoram*

Put the hare or rabbit either into a bowl or jug, cover with a mixture of water and vinegar and the remaining ingredients. Leave in a cool place for 1 or 2 days. Drain and wipe dry before using.

*50g (2oz) butter
50ml (2fl oz) olive oil
Juice 1/2 large lemon
90ml (3fl oz) brandy
450ml (3/4 pint) chicken stock
1 bay leaf*

*1/2 teaspoon cinnamon
12–15 good-sized walnuts
Salt and pepper
25g (1oz) plain flour
6 slices fried bread*

Shell, peel and crush the walnuts. Heat the butter and olive oil together, then add the hare or rabbit and lightly brown it. Add the lemon juice and the brandy, stirring carefully all the while, and, when all this has been absorbed, add the chicken stock (or water), bay leaf, cinnamon, salt and pepper. Cover and cook very gently until the meat is really tender. Hares should have long, slow cooking. Just before it is ready, add the crushed walnuts and the flour and continue cooking until the sauce has become quite thick. Have ready a slice of fried bread on each plate, spread this with some of the sauce, put a piece of the hare or rabbit on each slice, then add remaining sauce. If watercress is available, this makes an excellent garnish.

Greek cooking

Hare in White Wine Sauce

Layos Me Saltsa

1 good-sized hare or rabbit
From some celery, onion, carrot,
 leeks, parsley and equal parts
 of water and vinegar make a
 marinade, enough to cover
 the hare or rabbit
Plain flour
Olive oil for frying

Salt and pepper
750ml (1 1/4 pints) dry white wine
2–3 slices streaky bacon
6–8 small, whole onions
6 tablespoons tomato purée
1 bay leaf
150ml (1/4 pint) brandy
1 clove chopped garlic (optional)

Joint the hare or rabbit after thoroughly washing and cleaning it. Put it into the marinade and leave overnight. Next day remove it from the marinade, wipe the pieces dry, roll in seasoned flour and fry in deep, very hot fat until brown. Take from the frying pan and put into a large saucepan. Pour off most of the fat from the pan and leave just enough to fry 25g (1oz) of flour until it is brown but not scorched. Gradually pour in the white wine, stirring all the time, let it come to the boil, then pour it through a strainer over the meat. Add the bacon, onions (peeled and left whole), garlic (if used), tomato purée, bay leaf, salt and pepper. Cover the pan and cook over a medium heat until the hare or rabbit is tender. (Or all of this can be put into a casserole and baked in the oven.) Before serving discard the bay leaf, cut the bacon in small pieces and stir in the brandy.

The Greeks produce their own brandy, most of which is very good. So, although adding brandy may be expensive for some of us, for the Greeks it is not so. Therefore, brandy may be optional, but it does add to the flavour. If you cannot get Greek brandy try Cyprus brandy.

Hare Stew

Layos Stifatho

1 medium-sized hare or rabbit
12 small onions (whole)
225ml (8fl oz) Tomato Sauce (or juice)
2 cloves
1.2 litres (2 pints) water
50ml (2fl oz) olive oil

1–2 cloves chopped garlic
Few currants or seedless raisins
1 bay leaf
Salt and pepper
A little sugar

You can dispense with the garlic if you prefer or add more small onions, there is no hard and fast rule. In Athens, instead of cloves they use a round black seed with a clove flavour, but the two are interchangeable.

Wash the hare or rabbit and cut it into serving pieces. Arrange in a baking dish, add remaining ingredients, blending them well together. Cover tightly and cook at 150°C/300°F/Gas 2 for several hours, the longer the better. Give an occasional stir, being careful not to break the meat. Preferably serve with mashed potato although a famous Greek general told me mashed potato is a very 'sissy' kind of food, 'fit only for the aged and toothless'.

Greek cooking

Roast Rabbit with Marjoram Sauce

Kouneli Riyanato

1 rabbit	1 tablespoon chopped fresh marjoram
Juice 2 large lemons	1–2 cloves chopped garlic
125ml (4fl oz) olive oil	Salt and pepper

Prepare the rabbit and soak it in salt and water for 1 hour to remove all the blood. Drain it thoroughly and wipe it dry with a cloth. Put the rabbit in a baking tin into a really hot oven (230°C/450°F/Gas 8), quickly brown it, then reduce the oven heat to 150°C/300°F/Gas 2. Beat the olive oil and lemon juice together until thoroughly blended, then add the chopped marjoram, crushed garlic, salt and pepper. Pour this mixture over the rabbit and continue to bake until the rabbit is tender. Baste from time to time with the sauce from the pan. Take the rabbit from the pan, mix the drippings with the remaining sauce, add a little flour to thicken and just a little stock or water. Stir this into a gravy on top of the stove and serve with the rabbit.

Failing marjoram, fresh parsley goes extremely well with rabbit and, I think, plenty of parsley can be used.

Ragout of Rabbit

Kouneli Stifatho

There is a legend concerning this kind of cooking, bound up, as Greek legends so often are, with mountains and bandits. The story is that some bandits were in hiding near a mountain village and sniffed the delicious aroma coming from a nearby cottage, where a rabbit or two were simmering in a pot on the usual outdoor stove. The bandit chief commanded his men to go and fetch that pot of stew and, according to the legend, the leader ate the whole lot himself while his fellow bandits looked enviously on. But, the legend also adds, the leader, in gratitude for such a fine meal, spared the village from plundering, which must have been grand for all but the cook who was left without a meal to serve her hungry family.

Poultry and Game
Poulerika ke Kyniyi

The main distinction of the *stifatho* is that the meat is always literally smothered with small onions and well-seasoned with garlic and spices. It is cooked without any other vegetable, it requires no accompaniment and is served with Greek brown bread and always a bottle or so of red wine (preferably retsina). Even children must drink wine with *stifatho* as it helps the digestion. There are some Greeks who insist that only rabbit should be used for a *stifatho* but I have had *stifatho* of all kinds served to me, made with beef, hare or even lamb chops.

There are no absolute quantities one can give for this recipe, it is all a matter of taste. Essential details only are important.

Clean and joint one good-sized rabbit. Heat about 100g (4oz) of butter and lightly brown the pieces. Take from the pan and keep hot. In the same pan fry and brown 900g–1.4kg (2–3lb) of small, peeled but whole onions and 3 or 4 chopped cloves of garlic. Return the rabbit pieces to the pan, add about 300ml (1/2 pint) of thick, fresh Tomato Sauce (or tinned tomato soup) and 300ml (1/2 pint) of either dry white wine or white wine vinegar. Stir all this thoroughly, add a clove or so, a piece of cinnamon stick, some chopped fresh parsley, salt, pepper, 1–2 bay leaves and enough water to cover. Simmer over a low heat, tightly covered, for at least 3 hours, peek from time to time to see if there is still enough liquid and if not, stir in enough to keep the sauce thick but not like a gravy. Cover again and continue simmering. The sauce when served with the rabbit and onions should be as thick as a purée. This kind of dish improves if prepared in advance, left to stand for some time and then reheated.

I find that if plenty of finely chopped fresh parsley is sprinkled over the fried rabbit when it is taken out of the pan, the flavour is better.

Greek cooking

Rabbit with Cream

Kouneli Me Kaïmaki

A recipe from Salonika.

1 rabbit
600ml (1 pint) fresh double cream
75–100g (3–4oz) butter
Salt and pepper

600ml (1 pint) vinegar
1 bay leaf
3 cloves

Clean the rabbit and joint into serving pieces. Leave it for 2 hours marinating in the vinegar. Heat the butter, wipe the pieces of rabbit dry and fry them until brown in the hot butter. Sprinkle with salt and pepper and pour the vinegar over them. Continue cooking until the rabbit is quite tender. Add the cream, bay leaf and cloves and simmer gently for another 20 minutes. Just before serving, remove the bay leaf and cloves.

For people who think they do not like rabbit because of its appearance, it can be boned or cut to disguise its look and no announcement made.

Greek cream or *kaïmaki* is thick, so thick it can be sliced. The nearest equivalent is Devonshire cream.

Partridge with Olives and Celery

Perthikes Me Elies Ke Selino

Small birds, partridge, snipe, etc, are fairly easily available in most parts of the Mediterranean.

2–3 partridges	4 peeled and chopped tomatoes
2 heads celery	Butter or olive oil for frying
75g (3oz) stoned, green Greek olives	Salt

First simmer the olives for 10 minutes in their own juice. Clean the celery and chop it into small pieces. Heat enough butter to fry the partridges until brown, then add the celery and the olives, the tomatoes and enough water to just cover. Add salt and cook until tender. Cut the birds into halves, arrange on a platter and pour the sauce over them.

Greek cooking

Stuffed Turkey

Yemistes Yallopoules

Many Athenians assured me they like to eat turkey at Christmas and although the actual method of cooking does not vary much from the British, some of the Greek stuffings are rather more enterprising. In this recipe I shall also explain how one should prepare and roast the turkey because it is simpler if trying out a new stuffing recipe to have the whole process of roasting to hand.

1 turkey, about 5.4–6.4kg (12–14lb)	Salt and pepper
1 lemon	Butter

Wash the bird in cold water, pat dry inside and out, rub with salt, pepper, lemon and a little melted butter. Leave for 30 minutes while you cook your stuffing.

Meat Stuffing I

175g (6oz) minced lamb	50–75g (2–3oz) butter
1 turkey liver, minced	1 tablespoon pine nuts
1 lamb's liver, minced	600ml (1 pint) chicken stock
450g (1lb) boiled, peeled and	100g (4oz) soft breadcrumbs
broken chestnuts	2 sour apples
100g (4oz) long-grain rice	Salt and pepper
2 finely chopped onions	Melted butter

Peel the apples and chop them into small pieces. Heat the butter and fry the onions until they begin to change colour, then add the minced meat and simmer gently for 15 minutes. Add the minced heart and liver, the chestnuts and pine nuts and simmer for another 5 minutes. Add the chicken stock and bring this to the boil. Add the rice and cook quickly for 10 minutes, then add the lamb's liver, breadcrumbs and apples. Stir well.

To stuff the turkey slit the skin at the back of the neck and cut off the neck down to the turkey's shoulders. Lightly fill the breast cavity, remembering the stuffing always swells and too much swelling might cause the neck skin of the turkey to burst. Sew (or pin with a skewer) the neck flap to the back of the turkey. Just as lightly, fill the body cavity and sew or you could skewer this together.

Tie the legs to the tail and fix the wings snugly to the body, do not bring the cord across the breast for it marks the skin. Rub the turkey with salt, pepper and melted butter, place it in a large shallow pan and roast at 190°C/375°F/Gas 5 for about 4½ hours. Weigh the turkey when stuffed and roast it according to *this* weight, 1 hour for each kilogramme.

If you have made too much stuffing for your turkey it can be roasted in the tin and served with the turkey. Or it can be made into rissoles, dipped into beaten egg and breadcrumbs and served as a garnish. Greeks prefer to have plenty of stuffing so that it can be cooked separately and served with the turkey.

Meat Stuffing II

1 turkey liver, minced
1–2 medium-sized onions,
 finely chopped
225–350g (8–12oz) toasted breadcrumbs
450g (1lb) roasted, peeled and broken
 chestnuts

6–8 stoned black olives
2–3 chopped sticks celery
Butter for frying
Salt and pepper
Chicken stock
75g (3oz) sultanas or
 seedless raisins

Heat about 75g (3oz) of butter and just brown the onions. Add the liver, simmer for a few minutes, then stir in the breadcrumbs. Add the remaining dry ingredients, then the stock. Stir this all together with some care, let it come to the boil but cool it before stuffing the turkey. About 300ml (½ pint) of chicken stock should be sufficient. If this does not seem enough, cautiously add some more, but the stuffing must be neither too moist nor too dry. Exact measurements are rather difficult to give. Some shelled, peeled and crushed walnuts may also be added.

Greek cooking

Meat Stuffing III

This is very straightforward.

900g (2lb) chestnuts
2 large, chopped onions
25–50g (1–2oz) butter
2 tablespoons tomato purée
300ml (1/2 pint) chicken or turkey stock

450g (1lb) moist breadcrumbs
Handful chopped fresh parsley or
   fresh mint
Salt and pepper

Roast the chestnuts until they are easy to peel, then cook them in water until the inner skin comes off easily. Crush them. Heat the butter and fry the onions until they begin to change colour. Add the tomato purée, stock, salt, pepper and parsley (or mint) and simmer gently for 15 minutes. Add the breadcrumbs and the chestnuts and mix thoroughly. Cook for another 5 minutes, then stuff the turkey.

Meat Stuffing IV

450g (1lb) minced lamb
225g (8oz) long-grain rice
3 large, finely chopped onions
100g (4oz) butter
1 teaspoon ground cinnamon
2 tablespoons tomato purée

900ml (1½ pints) chicken or
*   turkey stock*
1 turkey liver, finely chopped
Salt and pepper
Finely chopped fresh mint to taste

Heat the butter and fry the onions and when they begin to change colour add the meat and liver. Simmer for 10 minutes. Add the tomato purée (diluted with some of the stock), stock, mint, cinnamon, salt and pepper. Bring to the boil, add the rice and cook over a moderate heat for 10 minutes. The rice will continue cooking while inside the roasting turkey so that 10 minutes is ample time.

Greek cooking

Vegetables
Lahanika

Vegetables have always held an important position in Greek cooking and generally they are used with intelligence and variety.

The Greeks make a main dish from a mixture of vegetables, in much the same way as the French do, although their methods of cooking vegetables are very un-French. Even in the days of ancient Greece, of Achilles and Ulysses, we read that often the most conspicuous dishes at state banquets were those consisting of vegetables.

Alexander must have been extremely fond of vegetables for he was for ever finding new ones and bringing them back to Greece and trying them out on his troops. Onions he found in Egypt, tried them, and decided they might be good to inspire martial ardour among his fighting men. (Indians are convinced that the onion arouses other ardours, and many of them ban it from their kitchens.) It was Alexander who discovered for Europe the haricot bean. Busily conquering bits of India he came across it, tried it out, found it good and brought back samples to grow in Greece. The Greeks have cultivated its various uses to far greater effect than the Indians, who seem to have pretty well forgotten all about their ancient haricot. In return for the haricot, Alexander, who must have been as interested in food as he was in warring, gave the Indians their first vines. But the Indians have neglected these even more than the haricot bean.

Oddly enough the cabbage has a long history and a proud one. In ancient times it was not the much maligned and neglected thing it often is today. The ancient Egyptians rated it so highly they raised altars to it. Both the Greeks and the Romans thought it a sovereign remedy against drunkenness. Athenaeus quoted Eubulus as crying:

Wife, quick! some cabbage boil, of virtues healing,
That I may rid me of this seedy feeling.

Vegetables
Lahanika

And it had other virtues. Erasistratus considered it a positive cure for paralysis and even in those far-off days it was never cooked in plain salted water, but with a number of spices including cumin, caraway, pepper and fresh coriander.

Leeks were also popular, considered as a cure-all for many diseases, often cooked with cabbage, olives, beetroot, beans and other vegetables. And talking of beetroot, they have long been served in Greece with a simple dressing of oil and lemon or a garlic sauce.

So many of the vegetables in vogue today had their origin in Greece and the Mediterranean generally. Artichokes, turnips and radishes, all these were known to the ancient Greeks, and naturally still are to the modern.

But Greeks are almost as fond of wild vegetables as they are of the cultivated kind and it is still a feature of Greek family life to go from time to time in due season to the mountains to collect the wild herbs and vegetables. Among these was the wild artichoke (still available), wild chicory and a type of wild spinach. There are dandelions, much used for stomach troubles among the country people, and, of course, there was, and still is, every kind of wild herb. These the industrious Greek cook arranges and dries or uses as long as they remain fresh. And while searching for vegetables and herbs the Greeks may look for snails and put them into a sack in which flour has been generously sprinkled, to take away the ooziness of the snails. These sacks of snails, even today, are often carried for long distances to be turned later into succulent island meals, for snails are more popular in the islands than on the mainland.

Greek cooking

Stuffed Vine Leaves

Dolmathes

In Greece, fresh vine leaves are available from spring to the end of autumn. After that they are kept, pliable and ready for use, preserved in brine in large tubs, and are sold in all the delicatessen stores. Tinned vine leaves are now readily available. As an alternative, I would recommend using the leaves of the beet or very large spinach leaves. Lettuce leaves can be used but I do not think they are as good as either those of the beet or spinach for they are inclined to disintegrate easily.

Stuffed vine leaves may be eaten hot or cold but the method of preparation for the cold and hot stuffings is different. If using cold, you must use olive oil, otherwise there will be the flavour of congealed butter or fat. Also, it is better to prepare the *dolmathes* the day before they are required and keep them in a cool place, but not in the refrigerator.

Dolmathes are really not difficult to prepare and their flavour is delicious. They are usually served as an appetizer with drinks, at a table and sitting down. They are rather difficult to cope with as a cocktail snack, even though one usually eats *dolmathes* with one's fingers. They make an excellent and unusual hors-d'oeuvre.

50–60 vine leaves	*600ml (1 pint) vegetable stock or water*
Hot or cold rice stuffing	*Juice ½ lemon*
(see page 122)	*1 tablespoon tomato purée*

Take the leaves, whether from a tub of brine or from a tin, and drop them quickly into hot water. Then spread them out on a table and select all the best ones. On to each put a teaspoon of rice stuffing. Roll the leaf into a neat little roll, roughly 5cm (2in) long and about 2.5cm (1in) across, to look like a small, fat sausage. Tuck in the edges of the leaf as you roll.

Cover the bottom of a thick-bottomed pan with vine leaves, any torn leaves can be used for this, then arrange a layer of *dolmathes*, packing them tightly to prevent movement while cooking. Between each layer of *dolmathes* arrange another layer of leaves. When all are in the pan, add the vegetable stock or water mixed with the tomato purée and the lemon juice, cover with a plate, this also is to prevent the *dolmathes* from moving, then cover the pan with its lid. Cook very slowly for about 2 hours.

The quantity of rice stuffing given in the recipe is for about 40 *dolmathes*. My own experience is that most people can eat from 4 to 6, for they are very small.

If serving the *dolmathes* hot, remove them from the pan and put into a warm oven while you make a sauce from the liquid in which they have been cooked. This consists of merely straining it and removing any bits of leaf. Some cooks stir a little yoghurt into the sauce, adding a flavour I heartily recommend.

If serving the *dolmathes* cold, leave them in the pan until they are quite cold. Then remove them carefully on to a platter and leave them until next day, or until really cold. Serve without sauce.

The secret of making successful *dolmathes* is to make them as small as possible and with not too much wrapping.

Rice and Meat Stuffing for Hot Dolmathes only

Yemissis Me Kreas Ke Rizi

450g (1lb) minced lamb
100g (4oz) long-grain rice
2 medium finely chopped onions
450ml (3/4 pint) vegetable stock
* (or water)*

1 tablespoon chopped fresh parsley
A little fresh sage
Salt and pepper
4 tablespoons olive oil

Heat the oil in a large saucepan and lightly fry the onions, meat and parsley, then add the rice. Fry for another 5 minutes. Add the vegetable stock or water, the seasonings and the sage. (You can also add chopped fresh mint.) Cook over the lowest possible heat for 15 minutes, by which time the rice should have absorbed all the liquid.

As soon as the stuffing is cool enough to handle, it is ready for use.

Greek cooking

Rice Stuffing for Cold Dolmathes

Yemissis Me Rizi

For this stuffing you *must* use olive oil. It is, I think, the only cooking oil which, when served cold, does not become thick, cloying and unpleasant.

225g (8oz) long-grain rice
150ml (1/4 pint) olive oil
300ml (1/2 pint) boiling water
1 tablespoon tomato purée
2 chopped onions
1 tablespoon pine nuts

1 tablespoon currants
1 tablespoon chopped fresh mint
1 teaspoon chopped fresh sage
1 tablespoon sugar
Salt and pepper

Heat the olive oil and lightly fry the onions. Add the rice and cook over a low heat for 20 minutes, stirring almost all the time. Add the water, the tomato purée, currants, pine nuts, sage, mint, salt and pepper. Stir well, cover and continue cooking over a low heat for yet another 20 minutes. Stir in the sugar. By this time all the liquid should be absorbed but if not, pour away any which remains. Leave to cool in the pan before using.

Meat and Celery Stuffing

Yemissis Me Kreas Ke Selino

350g (12oz) minced lamb or beef
75g (3oz) long-grain rice
1 large finely chopped onion
2 stalks finely chopped celery
Handful finely chopped fresh
  parsley

4 tablespoons olive oil
1/2 teaspoon ground cinnamon
Salt and pepper
Breadcrumbs

Enough to fill 6–8 large tomatoes, small aubergines, courgettes or peppers.

Scoop out the pulp from the vegetables which you propose to stuff. Chop this finely. Mix the meat, rice, onion, pulp, salt, pepper, 3 tablespoons olive oil, cinnamon, parsley and celery.

As this is a stuffing using both uncooked rice and meat, at least an hour of slow baking should be allowed. It must also be remembered that rice swells in cooking and that the vegetables you are stuffing should never be more than three quarters filled.

See stuffed peppers and stuffed tomatoes for further directions.

Greek cooking

Stuffing for Vegetables
(Without Meat)

Yemissis Horis Kreas

2 finely chopped onions
100g (4oz) long-grain rice
3 tablespoons pine nuts
Handful finely chopped fresh
  parsley

1 tablespoon finely chopped fresh dill
225ml (8fl oz) olive oil
Salt and pepper

The above quantity is sufficient to fill 12 tomatoes, or about 10 large aubergines or courgettes. It is hard to give exact quantities in such recipes.

First scoop out the pulp from the vegetables you are wanting to stuff, and chop it finely. Heat the olive oil, then lightly fry the onions. When they begin to change colour add the vegetable pulp. Stir this for 5 minutes, add the rice, nuts, parsley, dill, salt and pepper and cook gently for 10 minutes. The stuffing is then ready to be filled into the empty vegetable cases. Only three quarters fill the cases as the rice will continue to swell. See Stuffed Tomatoes.

Artichokes

Anginares

When the Greeks talk of artichokes they mean what we call globe artichokes, and botanically they are correct. There are two other so-called artichokes, the Jerusalem and the Chinese, but these, botanists declare, are not true artichokes at all. The Jerusalem belongs to the sunflower or *helianthus* species, and the Chinese is a *stachys*. This information I find far less interesting than the legendary origin of the true artichoke, said to come from one of the Aegean Islands called Zinari where lived a beautiful girl named Cynara. She was so beautiful that a jealous God (or Goddess) turned her into a globe artichoke, which is of the species *cynara*.

However, botanists have another, unhappily more prosaic, story which states that the artichoke is the result of the study and skill of botanists who worked on the cardoon and the common thistle, creating a hybrid.

A very long time ago Theophrastus, a Greek writer, wrote of the artichoke, insisting that it was first grown in Sicily and not in the Aegean Islands, which does, I fear, knock my legend for six. He stated, 'they are edible when picked, are slightly bitter and men preserve them in brine'. And he had the reputation of being a reliable reporter.

The Romans also liked artichokes and at one time they were one of the most expensive items of their diet. At a much later period Catharine de Medici took artichokes with her to France. It was about then that the artichoke lost its reputation, like the onion and garlic, and became a by-word for its 'heating' or aphrodisiacal qualities, perhaps because of the Medicis.

By the seventeenth century the artichoke had won its way, however, into English cooking and artichoke pie was considered a famous delicacy. Ben Jonson in his book, *Every Man in His Humour*, mentions the 'artichoke that has pepper and salt in and needs no more'.

There are several varieties of globe artichokes, at least a dozen and possibly more. They grow extremely well in England. Apparently our foggy, damp climate with not too much sun suits the artichoke well. One gardener told me the reward for his gardening efforts in artichokes was fresh, young artichokes crisp to the tooth with the delicate sweet-bitter flavour unimpaired.

Greek cooking

Boiled Globe Artichokes

Anginares Vrastes

Rinse as many artichokes as required in cold, salted water, pull off any discoloured leaves, then trim the remaining leaves of each artichoke with a pair of scissors, cutting off about 1cm (1/2in) from the top. Trim round the base with a knife. Tie the leaves together with cotton, bring this down under the artichoke and affix quite firmly a thin slice of lemon to the base. (This is to keep the base white, or as near as possible white, for it is really a soft shade of green.) Have ready a large pan of boiling, salted water and drop the artichokes into this. Cook steadily for 45 minutes, or longer if they are still not tender. To test for tenderness pull away a leaf. If it comes off easily the artichokes are cooked.

Remove the cotton and the lemon and turn the artichokes upside down to drain. Serve with hot butter or a Lemon and Mustard Sauce (see page 168).

Most people who like artichokes can eat 2 medium-sized artichokes, or for that matter 2 large ones.

Try adding 1 whole clove of garlic, 1 tablespoon of olive oil and 2 tablespoons of vinegar to the pan when cooking artichokes. It may not be strictly Greek but it adds a certain piquancy to the flavour of the artichokes.

Artichokes – Constantinople Style

Anginares à La Polita

A very popular dish among Greeks when the artichokes are first in season.

12 medium-sized globe artichokes
2–3 thickly sliced carrots
12 small onions
450g (1lb) small potatoes,
  preferably new
225ml (8fl oz) olive oil

1 tablespoon finely chopped
  fresh dill
4 finely chopped spring onions,
  green stalks as well
Juice 4 lemons
1 tablespoon plain flour
Salt and pepper

Thoroughly wash the artichokes, cut off the stems to about 2.5cm (1in) of the globe, remove the coarser outer leaves and cut off 6mm (1/4in) from the tips of the remaining leaves. Cut each artichoke in half and scrape away the fuzz or choke. Leave the artichokes for about 15 minutes in salt water flavoured with the juice of 1 lemon. Drain well.

Put the artichokes, the carrots, potatoes (peeled or scraped), onions, dill, spring onions, salt and pepper into a pan and just cover with water. Beat the olive oil with the remaining lemon juice, add the flour, and when this mixture is well-blended add it to the pan. Cover and cook very slowly for 1 hour, or until the artichokes are very tender. Serve them in the sauce in which they are cooked, garnished with the vegetables.

Many Greeks prefer to cook the artichokes whole but then they must be very young, too young for the fuzzy choke to have become coarse. Baby artichokes are quite delicious.

Greek cooking

Artichokes à La Grèque
(Greek-American Style)

Anginares Hellenikes

12 small globe artichokes
6 very small peeled onions
1 clove garlic
125ml (4fl oz) dry white wine

Juice 1 lemon
50ml (2fl oz) olive oil
Salt and pepper to taste

Prepare the artichokes as in preceding recipe, then let them stand for 10 minutes in a bowl of boiling water. Drain. Put into a pan the onions, garlic, wine, lemon juice, olive oil, salt, pepper and finally the artichokes. Add boiling water to cover and cook them for 25 to 30 minutes, or until you can pull off the leaves easily. Take out the artichokes, turn them upside down to drain, then arrange on a dish. Reduce the liquid in which they have been cooked to about half or just a little less, add, if required, a little more salt and pepper and pour this, while still hot, over the artichokes. Leave until cold before serving.

This is the Greek-American version of *Anginares à la Polita*.

Artichoke Bottoms and Broad Beans

Anginares Me Koykia

For this recipe you can use tinned artichoke bottoms.

Cook in the usual manner about 900g (2lb) shelled fresh or frozen broad beans, strain them and keep a little of the water in which they were cooked.

Heat 3 tablespoons of olive oil in a pan and stir into it about 1 tablespoon of cornflour. Add 600ml (1 pint) of the liquid from the beans, the strained juice of 1 lemon, a handful of finely chopped fresh parsley, and blend this mixture thoroughly. Add the artichoke bottoms and the beans and simmer until the artichokes are hot.

Serve the vegetables in the sauce. It is a good idea to make the sauce in a fireproof dish which can also be used as a serving dish as this does away with the business of removing the artichoke bottoms and possibly breaking them.

Stuffed Artichokes

Anginares Yemistes

A popular dish with Greeks during the week preceding Easter.

8–10 globe artichokes
Juice 1 large lemon
150ml (1/4 pint) olive oil

450g (1lb) shelled broad beans,
 these can be fresh or frozen

Stuffing

1 medium, finely chopped onion
2 chopped garlic cloves
3 finely chopped stalks celery
Bunch finely chopped fresh parsley

Handful finely chopped fresh dill
1 teaspoon finely chopped fresh mint
Salt and pepper

Thoroughly wash the artichokes and cut off enough of the stems to make them 'sit' firmly when served. With a sharp pair of scissors, cut off about 1cm (1/2in) of the tips of the leaves and sprinkle the artichokes well with lemon juice. Cook until almost tender. Drain, cool and then remove enough of the centre to be able to scrape away at the fuzzy heart or choke.

Make the Stuffing. Heat a tablespoon of olive oil and lightly fry the onion and the garlic. Add the chopped herbs, celery, salt and pepper. Take from the pan and mix in a bowl with half the remaining oil. Insert this mixture into the leaves of the artichokes. Put the artichokes into a saucepan, add water almost to cover, and the remaining oil, and cook slowly for 30 minutes. Add the beans (if using fresh) and continue to cook for another 25 minutes or until they are tender.

If using frozen beans cook them only for the length of time indicated on the packet. Stuffed artichokes may be served hot or cold.

Fried Artichokes

Anginares Tiyanites

6–8 medium globe artichokes	100g (4oz) breadcrumbs
2 eggs	Salt and pepper to taste
Juice 1 lemon	

Strip off the outer, tougher leaves of the artichokes, then cut each one lengthways into halves and scrape out the choke. Cover with water and lemon juice and leave them for about 2 hours to remove all the tiny insects which harbour within the leaves. Boil for about 30 minutes or steam for about 40 minutes, longer if the heads are large. Drain thoroughly.

Beat the eggs until light, adding one tablespoon of warm (not hot) water. Dip the drained artichoke halves first into beaten egg, then breadcrumbs, again in egg, and then fry them in deep, very hot oil until a golden brown. Can be served as a main dish or with poultry or meat. Many Greek cooks mix grated cheese with the breadcrumbs.

As my recipes are from varying sources there may appear certain inconsistencies. For example, this is the only recipe with artichokes which suggests soaking them in order to remove possible insects. Other Greek cooks prefer to remove all the leaves after washing the artichokes, boiling only the bottoms until just tender and then, with great care, drying these on a clean towel before they are fried.

Aubergines

Melitzanes

Aubergine, or egg plant, as the Americans call it, has a large and enthusiastic following in many parts of the world. The Italians, French, Greeks and all the Balkan peoples use it extensively. So do the Indians, who call it *brinjal*.

There are several varieties, ranging from almost black to ivory white and, in shape, from tiny balls to long sausage shapes. They were introduced into England in the nineteenth century but as this was before the days of greenhouses gardeners found them almost impossible to grow; they do require some warmth. The name aubergine is supposed to have been derived from an Arabic word meaning 'peach'.

There are some general rules for cooking aubergines. First, they contain a large percentage of water, a fact which can cause trouble to the unwary cook, for when an aubergine is peeled or cut the watery content is not apparent at all. Before frying aubergine I usually sprinkle the slices generously with salt then pile them on to a platter and cover with a plate. If left for an hour or so, much of the water disappears. Before using, the slices should be dried and then fried in deep boiling oil, otherwise they will not be crisp. Properly fried, thick slices of aubergine are soft inside and delightfully crisp on the outside.

Greek cooking

Aubergines with Onions and Tomatoes

Melitzanes Yahni

Slice 2 or 3 medium-sized aubergines, sprinkle with salt and press between 2 plates. Leave for an hour or so, then wipe dry.

Heat plenty of olive oil in a pan and quickly brown the aubergine slices. When these are ready, take them from the pan, pour off most of the oil, then brown one sliced onion. Return the aubergine slices plus plenty of chopped fresh parsley, peeled and thinly sliced tomatoes, a bay leaf and some slivers of garlic. Cook very slowly for 45 minutes. Serve hot.

This is not unlike the Provençale dish of ratatouille. Some Greek cooks prefer not to fry the aubergine slices before putting them on to the browned onions. It is less rich this way.

Enough for 3 or 4 people, depending on the size of the aubergines.

Stuffed Aubergines

Melitzanes Yemistes

4 medium-sized aubergines
2 large chopped tomatoes
1–2 cloves chopped garlic
1–2 chopped onions

Handful finely chopped fresh parsley
3 tablespoons olive oil
Salt and pepper

Put the aubergines into a large pan, cover with water and bring to the boil. Cook for 5 minutes, drain and pat dry. Cut 3 or 4 slits, lengthways, into each aubergine. Mix the tomatoes, garlic, onions, parsley, salt and pepper and push as much of the mixture as will go, into the slits. Rub the aubergines with olive oil and place them in a baking tin. Add 300ml (1/2 pint) of hot water and bake at 190°C/375°F/Gas 5 1½ hours, or until tender.

Sufficient for 2 or 4 people, according to the size of the aubergines.

Stuffed Aubergine Imam Bayildi

Imam Bayildi

Strictly speaking this is a Turkish recipe but the Greeks have taken it into their kitchens. Some Greeks even claim it as a Moorish dish. An amusing story is connected with it; in fact, there are many versions of the same story. Once there was a famous Turkish imam (a priest) who was particularly fond of aubergine. Naturally his wife tried to give him aubergine as often as she could, always thinking up new ways of cooking it. One day she prepared some in the manner of this recipe and her delighted imam found them so good that he swooned in ecstasy. Since then both her recipe and the story have become legendary, hence the name, which means 'fainting imam'.

Two other reasons given for the swooning are that the imam was a mean man and fainted when he saw the vast quantity of oil used, or that he fainted because the richness overpowered him.

6 long aubergines	Plenty finely chopped fresh parsley
3 chopped onions	Salt and pepper
3 large chopped and peeled tomatoes	300ml (1/2 pint) vegetable stock or water
2 sliced tomatoes	300ml (1/2 pint) olive oil,
Juice 1 lemon	Chopped garlic to taste
	1–2 teaspoons sugar (optional)

Cut off and discard the green end of the aubergines and make 3 slits in each stretching from end to end. Do not peel them. Sprinkle a little salt inside the slits and leave for 20 minutes. Then gently squeeze each aubergine to rid it of excess water. Heat the oil and fry the aubergines for 5 minutes or until they begin to wilt, turning 2 or 3 times. Take them from the pan and put aside until required. In the same pan fry the onions until they are a golden brown. Also take these from the pan and put into a basin.

Add to the onions the chopped tomatoes, parsley, garlic, salt and pepper. Mix all this well together and stuff the mixture into the slits of the aubergines. Arrange the aubergines in a baking dish and pour over them the olive oil in which you fried the onions. Cover the aubergines with the sliced tomatoes, pour in the stock, the lemon juice, sugar (if used) and a little more salt. Cover the pan and bake at 190°C/375°F/Gas 5 until the aubergines are quite soft. Leave to cool before taking them from the pan and then serve

continued

quite cold. At least, this is the Balkan way of serving this dish. It is just as good served hot, I think even better.

Sugar is optional, being added merely to reduce the acidity of the tomatoes.

If, like the imam, you find this dish rather rich, do not swoon, but make a few alterations instead. For example, use half the quantity of olive oil and do not pre-fry either the onions or the aubergines. Instead, simply mix the vegetables with some of the oil, using the remainder for cooking.

But, if you do this, although you will have a palatable dish, it will not be a real *Imam Bayildi.*

Little Shoes (Stuffed Aubergines)

Papoutsakia

6 medium aubergines
100g (4oz) butter
1–2 finely chopped onions
175–225g (6–8oz) minced meat,
  (veal, lamb or beef)
125ml (4fl oz) tomato juice

1 tablespoon finely chopped
  fresh parsley
Salt and pepper
600ml (1 pint) Béchamel Sauce
  (see page 165)
Grated Parmesan cheese

Wash the aubergines and cut them in halves lengthways. Scoop out the pulp, chop this finely and fry the empty cases in a little butter until they begin to soften. Remove from the pan and arrange in a baking dish.

Add all but 25g (1oz) of the remaining butter to the frying pan. Heat this, then add the onions, brown them; add the meat, let this brown, then add the pulp, parsley, salt and pepper, and finally the tomato juice. Cook over a moderate heat until the mixture is fairly dry. Take it from the stove, leave until cool, then add grated Parmesan cheese to taste. Fill the empty cases with this mixture. Cover each with a layer of Béchamel Sauce and sprinkle with grated Parmesan cheese. Add about 125ml (4fl oz) of boiling water to the pan, and the remaining butter and bake at 190°C/375°F/Gas 5 until the sauce is brown and the aubergines soft, about 30 minutes. Serve hot.

Aubergine Fritters

Melitzanes Tiyanites

Slice as many aubergines as required, about 6mm (1/4in) thick. Sprinkle the slices with salt and put between two plates for 2 hours. Wipe free of salt and moisture, lightly coat in flour and fry in deep boiling olive oil until browned on both sides. Serve hot.

I recommend fried aubergine served with beaten yoghurt flavoured with crushed garlic. The aubergine should be very hot and the yoghurt cold, this is not Greek but typically Balkan.

Runner Beans

Fassolakia Freska

Trim as many runner beans as required, then break each into 2 or 3 pieces. Fry some onions in a little oil or butter until they begin to change colour. Add about a tablespoon of tomato purée, sufficient boiling water to cover, bring to the boil, add the beans and cook slowly for 45 minutes. Season with salt and pepper to taste.

To 900g (2lb) of beans 1 medium-sized onion would be sufficient. To be served as a main course.

Greek cooking

Green Beans with Tomatoes

Fassolakia Freska Me Domates

900g (2lb) French green beans
1 onion
450g (1lb) tomatoes
Chopped fresh parsley

About 225ml (8fl oz) olive oil
Salt and pepper
A little sugar

Peel and chop the tomatoes and the onion. Wash and trim the beans, snap them into halves if they are very long but do not slice them thinly. Heat the olive oil, lightly fry the onion, add the beans and simmer until they begin to soften. At this point add the tomatoes, salt, pepper and parsley, a little sugar and just enough water to cover. Continue to cook slowly until the beans are tender, about 40 minutes is the Greek timing.

Beans cooked in this way are usually served as a main course but they can be offered as an accompaniment to a meat dish. The amount of oil is probably rather excessive for the British palate but it can be reduced by half or even more. This quantity of beans would be enough for 4 people if served as a main course.

Not all Greek cooks use sugar when cooking tomatoes, its purpose is to reduce the acid content. Many modern Greek cooks are also beginning to disapprove of large quantities of olive oil being used and of pre-frying their vegetables before boiling them.

Braised Cabbage

Lahana Yahni

1 large Savoy cabbage
2 medium-sized, finely
  chopped onions
1–2 chopped stalks celery
2 chopped tomatoes

2 small, thinly sliced carrots
Salt and pepper to taste
A few capers
50g (2oz) olive oil

Discard the outer, coarse leaves and the stalks of the cabbage, and cut it into 8 pieces. Remove any really thick stem. Wash the cabbage thoroughly and drain. Heat the oil and lightly cook the onions, add the celery, tomatoes, carrots, salt and pepper and lastly the cabbage, with just enough water to prevent sticking or burning. Cook for 10 minutes, add the capers and continue to cook until the cabbage is tender.

The olive oil can be omitted if you like, the cabbage is still very good cooked with this mixture of vegetables.

Greek cooking

Stuffed Cabbage Leaves
(with pork and rice)

Lahana Dolmathes Me Hirino

1 very large Savoy cabbage	*Salt and pepper*
900g (2lb) minced pork	*1–2 teaspoons spice*
175g (6oz) long-grain rice	*Egg and Lemon Sauce*
50g (2oz) butter	* (see page 165)*
1 chopped onion	

The usual spice in this stuffing is aniseed, but caraway, cinnamon or any other spice may be used provided it matches with pork, and incidentally many Greeks feel that only a pork stuffing marries with cabbage. This is not my opinion. I have made cabbage *dolmathes* many times and found that all varieties of meat or meatless stuffings produce a very palatable dish.

Melt the butter and lightly fry the onions. Add the pork, rice, salt and pepper and the spice. Cook very slowly for about 10 minutes, stirring almost all the while. Take from the heat.

Cook the cabbage in boiling, salted water long enough to soften the leaves, 5 or 10 minutes. Drain and when cool enough to handle separate the leaves. Lay these flat on a table and trim the thick centre vein, this is to make the leaves more pliable. Put on to each leaf about a tablespoon of the meat mixture (the actual amount depends on the size of the leaf.) Roll each leaf carefully into a package, as described for vine leaf *dolmathes* on page 120. Arrange the *dolmathes* in a large shallow pan in neat rows and close together. If you need to make a second layer put spare cabbage leaves on top of the *dolmathes*, then arrange remaining *dolmathes* on top of the leaves. Add water to cover and cover with a plate to keep the *dolmathes* steady. Put on the lid of the saucepan and cook slowly for at least 1 hour. Remove the *dolmathes* carefully from the pan and serve hot with an Egg and Lemon Sauce which you can prepare while the *dolmathes* are cooking.

Sufficient for between 4 and 6 people, but it is difficult to say exactly since the cabbage leaves vary so much in size, appetites vary even more, and some people like to put more meat in the leaves, others less.

Stuffed Cabbage Leaves

Dolmathes Lahana

16 cabbage leaves
175g (6oz) long-grain rice
2 finely chopped onions
1–2 chopped cloves garlic
1 tablespoon pine nuts
1 tablespoon sultanas or
  currants

Pinch ground nutmeg or cinnamon
2–3 finely chopped tomatoes
Salt and pepper
3 tablespoons olive oil
Tomato juice and lemon juice
  (optional)
Plain flour or single cream

The cabbage leaves must be fairly large, whole and fresh, and as it takes only a minute or so to make them pliable it is better to make the stuffing first.

Heat the oil and fry the rice for 2 or 3 minutes, then add the onions, garlic, sultanas (or currants) and pine nuts. Stir almost all the while and let these ingredients cook slowly until a golden brown, but not too dark. Add the tomatoes, the nutmeg or cinnamon, salt and pepper. Continue simmering for about 5 minutes more. Put aside until required, but keep hot.

Blanch the cabbage leaves in boiling water to make them pliable. Spread the leaves out on a table and trim away the thick centre vein, this makes the leaves easier to roll. Put a small portion of the stuffing on to each leaf, roll it up carefully, tucking in the edges (as described for Vine Leaf *Dolmathes* on page 120). Pack the dolmathes close together in a saucepan, cover with salted water or tomato juice, sprinkle with lemon juice and place an upturned plate over them to keep them steady. If the *dolmathes* have plenty of space they will swim around and possibly break. Cover with the saucepan lid and cook very slowly for 45 minutes. Take the dolmathes from the pan when cooked, keep them hot while you thicken the sauce, this can be done with cream or with a flour and water paste. Serve the *dolmathes* and their sauce separately.

Greek cooking

Cauliflower Cooked in Tomato Juice

Kounoupithi Yahni

1 large cauliflower
2 large, finely chopped onions
450ml (3/4 pint) tomato juice
1–2 chopped cloves garlic

Handful finely chopped fresh parsley
Salt and pepper
50g (2oz) olive oil
Plain flour (optional)

Thoroughly wash the cauliflower, remove the coarse stalks and separate the flowerets. Heat the oil and fry the onions and the garlic until a golden brown, then add the tomato juice, salt, pepper and parsley and bring this to the boil. Add the cauliflower and cook it until tender. Serve the sauce separately, this can be thickened with flour.

Celeriac with Egg and Lemon Sauce

Selinorrizes Avgolemono

About 450g (1lb) celeriac
100g (4oz) butter
Salt and pepper

Egg and Lemon Sauce
(see page 165)

Wash and peel the celeriac and cut it into cubes. Heat the butter and brown the pieces, add salt and pepper and enough water or vegetable stock to cover. Cook until tender. Prepare the Egg and Lemon Sauce, using some of the liquid from the celeriac to thin it. Take the pan from the fire and pour the sauce into it, mixing it with the celeriac. Return it to the stove to reheat but take it off before the sauce actually boils. Cover and leave to 'settle' for 2 or 3 minutes, then serve hot.

Celery can be used in precisely the same manner as celeriac except that it takes half the time to cook.

Stewed Marrow or Squash I

Kolokithakia Yahni I

Many years ago, when I was in America for the first time, I was offered squash, Hubbard squash to be exact. I asked the waitress, 'What is squash?' and she replied (rather tersely, I thought), 'Squash is squash.' She was more or less right, squash is squash. With this particular recipe you can use pumpkin, cucumber, baby marrows, or custard marrows, etc.

450g (1lb) marrow or squash
50ml (2fl oz) olive oil
2 large chopped onions
1 tablespoon finely chopped
  fresh parsley

4 peeled and chopped tomatoes
125ml (4fl oz) water
Salt and pepper
Grated Cheddar cheese

Cut the marrow into 2.5cm (1in) cubes. If the vegetable is young there is no need to peel it first, scraping is enough, but this is a matter for personal preference. Heat the olive oil, lightly brown the onions, then add the tomatoes, salt, pepper, parsley and water. Cook for 5 minutes, stir until blended, then add the marrow, cover and cook slowly for about 30 minutes.

Serve hot with grated cheese.

When using marrows, ideally they should be small, not more than 12.5cm (5in) long and nicely plump. At this stage they have a delicate flavour.

Greek cooking

Stewed Marrow II

Kolokithakia Yahni II

900g (2lb) marrow (or similar squash)
450g (1lb) tomatoes
225g (8oz) finely chopped onions

Handful finely chopped
  fresh parsley
Salt and pepper to taste
125ml (4fl oz) olive oil

Peel the marrow, scrape out the seeds and cut the flesh into small pieces, roughly the size of an egg. Peel and chop the tomatoes into fairly small pieces.

Heat the oil, lightly brown the onions, add the tomatoes and when these are soft add the marrow, salt, pepper, parsley and a very little water, only enough to prevent the vegetables from burning. Bring to the boil, then cook more slowly until the marrow is tender but not a squashed mass.

Serve with a garlic sauce (see pages 166–7).

Enough for 6 people and meant to be served as a main course.

Marrow Pie (Greek-American)

Kolokithopita

900g (2lb) marrow
3 thinly sliced onions
125ml (4fl oz) finely chopped
  fresh parsley and fresh dill (mixed)

450g (1lb) sliced tomatoes
100g (4oz) soft breadcrumbs
125ml (4fl oz) olive oil
Salt and pepper

Scrape or peel the marrow and thickly slice it. Rub a baking tin with oil, cover the bottom with a layer of marrow, and spread with onion, tomato, breadcrumbs, salt, pepper, parsley and dill. Repeat this until all the ingredients are used up, with tomatoes as the top layer. Pour olive oil over the top, distributing it evenly. Bake at 190°C/375°F/Gas 5 for about 1 hour, longer if necessary, until all the vegetables are soft.

This quantity is sufficient for 6 people. I usually add also either some tomato juice or a little stock to the pie, as it can sometimes be a little dry.

Marrow Fritters

Kolokithokeftethes

700g (1½lb) marrow
1 large, finely chopped onion
3 tablespoons finely chopped
  fresh parsley
3 tablespoons grated Cheddar cheese

2 tablespoons melted butter
450g (1lb) soft breadcrumbs
2 eggs
Salt and pepper
Olive oil and butter for frying

Peel the marrow, scrape out the seeds, cut into halves and cook in boiling, salted water with the onion until soft. Drain absolutely free from water then mash until smooth. Put the mashed marrow into a mixing bowl, add salt and pepper, Cheddar cheese, breadcrumbs, the melted butter, then add the eggs without beating them first. Mix all this together and leave for 1 hour. Shape into rissoles, any size you like, and fry in a mixture of equal parts olive oil and butter until brown.

Enough for 4 to 6 people.

Greek cooking

Ladies Fingers Okra with Tomatoes

Bamies Me Domates

450g (1lb) ladies' fingers okra
6 peeled and chopped tomatoes
125ml (4fl oz) olive oil
125ml (4fl oz) vinegar

2 large chopped onions
Handful finely chopped fresh parsley
Salt and pepper

Wash the ladies' fingers, carefully trim off the stems, taking care not to cut into the flesh. Put them into a bowl, pour the vinegar over them and leave for 30 minutes. Rinse thoroughly.

Heat the olive oil and brown the onions, add the tomatoes and cook slowly for 5 minutes. Add the ladies' fingers, parsley, salt, pepper and enough hot water to cover. Cook slowly for 45 minutes.

The amount of oil can easily be reduced to half, which is better for the average non-Mediterranean palate. The reason for soaking the ladies' fingers in vinegar is to take away some of their stickiness. This is meant to be a main dish and not an accompanying vegetable to meat.

Stuffed Peppers

Piperies Yemistes

To stuff peppers, you can use any of the stuffings prepared for *dolmathes* or tomatoes. Cut around the stalks very carefully and remove them but put on one side, to be returned later as little lids. Carefully take out the cores and seeds and continue as for stuffed tomatoes, (see pages 150–1). Some cooks prefer to soften the peppers in boiling water before stuffing but usually the peppers become soft enough during cooking. Whether the peppers (capsicum) are green, red or yellow does not matter, the flavour is the same. However, variety in colour does add to the appearance of a dish of stuffed peppers. When serving stuffed vegetables I like to mix them in any case: tomatoes, aubergines, courgettes and peppers all appear at the same meal.

Potato Pie (Greek Shepherd's Pie)

Patates Purée Me Kreas

3–4 floury potatoes
450g (1lb) minced lamb or beef
2 minced onions

2 chopped cloves garlic
Butter
Salt and pepper

Cook the potatoes in their skins until very soft. As soon as they are cool enough to handle, peel and mash them until quite smooth. Add salt and pepper and enough butter to make the potatoes creamy. It is worthwhile taking the trouble to whip the potatoes with a wire whisk.

Heat a little butter in a pan, add the meat, stir it well, and as it begins to change colour add the garlic and the onions. Cook gently for about 10 or 15 minutes, add salt and pepper. The onions should become soft but not brown.

Rub a casserole lightly with butter, then spread it with half of the mashed potatoes. Cover with the meat mixture, then with the remainder of the potatoes. Dot the top with butter and bake at 190°C/375°F/Gas 5 until the potato has browned.

This is sufficient for between 5 to 6 people. Some Greeks add chopped tomatoes as well, cooking these with the meat and onions until soft.

Greek cooking

Potatoes Cooked with Tomatoes

Patates Yahni

There are many Greek vegetable dishes cooked in this manner, usually with olive oil, but butter or margarine may be substituted.

900g–1.4kg (2–3lb) potatoes
450g (1lb) chopped onions
450g (1lb) peeled and chopped
  tomatoes

125ml (4fl oz) olive oil
Salt and pepper

Wash and peel the potatoes and cut into uniform sizes. Heat the oil and fry the onions until they are a golden brown. Add the tomatoes, simmer until soft, then add the potatoes, salt and pepper and enough hot water to cover. Cook until the potatoes are soft and the sauce is thick.

Usually served as a main dish.

Potato Croquettes

Patates Kroketes

450g (1lb) potatoes
25g (1oz) butter
1 small, finely chopped onion
1/2 tablespoon finely chopped
  fresh parsley

Salt and pepper
50g (2oz) grated Cheddar cheese
2 well-beaten eggs
Olive oil for frying
Plain flour

Wash and cook the potatoes in their skins until very soft, peel as soon as possible and then mash them until smooth. Add the butter, onion, salt, pepper, parsley and 1 egg. With floured hands form this mixture into rounds, quite small; roll them in the remaining egg, coat with Cheddar cheese, then fry in deep, boiling oil until a golden brown. Serve very hot.

Potato croquettes are often served as appetizers with drinks.

Potato Omelette

Omeletta Me Patates

3 medium potatoes
4 eggs
A little grated Cheddar cheese

3 tablespoons grated onion
Butter or margarine
Salt and pepper

Wash and peel the potatoes and cut into very thin strips. Put enough butter into a frying pan and fry first the onion till a light brown, and then the potatoes. Beat the eggs, add the grated Cheddar cheese, salt and pepper and pour this mixture into the pan over the potatoes and onions. Continue to cook over a medium heat until the eggs have set.

This type of omelette is not folded but usually slid flat on to a hot plate for seeing. If you possess one of those frying pans which can also be used at table, all the better.

Spinach with Rice

Spanakorizo

900g (2lb) spinach
2 leeks (optional)
2 medium-sized onions

100g (4oz) long-grain rice
125ml (4fl oz) olive oil
Salt and pepper

Thoroughly wash the spinach and break it into small pieces. Clean and chop the remaining vegetables. Heat the olive oil, add the spinach and chopped vegetables and cook until brown. Add salt and pepper and continue cooking until the mixture is soft. Add 600ml (1 pint) of water, bring this to the boil, then add the rice and cook until the rice is tender, from 15 to 20 minutes.

If using the leeks, remember to use as much of the green part as possible.

Greek cooking

Spinach Pie with Cheese I

Spanakopita I

900g (2lb) spinach
1 tablespoon finely chopped fresh dill
2 tablespoons finely chopped
  fresh parsley
2–3 large, finely chopped onions

225g (8oz) mashed feta cheese
10 sheets of filo pastry
  (see pages 177–8)
225ml (8fl oz) olive oil
Salt and pepper

Thoroughly wash the spinach, chop it finely, sprinkle it with salt and pepper and leave it for 1 hour. Squeeze it to remove its bitter liquid. Heat the olive oil and fry the onions until brown, add the spinach and cook this until tender, stirring all the time. With a perforated spoon take it from the pan and put it into a bowl. Crumble the feta cheese into the bowl, add pepper, parsley and dill. Mix well. Let the olive oil cool.

Brush a roasting tin with oil and line it with 1 sheet of filo pastry. Brush this with oil, add 4 more sheets of pastry, brushing each with oil. Cover the last sheet with the spinach mixture, add the remaining pastry, each sheet brushed with oil. Score the top sheet into squares, using a sharp, pointed knife, sprinkle the top lightly with water, to prevent the pastry from curling upwards, and bake the pie at 190°C/375°F/Gas 5 until the top is a golden brown, about 40 minutes. Cool slightly before cutting into squares and serve either hot or cold.

If filo pastry is not available use flaky pastry and make a pie in the usual way.

Spinach Pie II

Spanakopita II

1.8kg (4lb) spinach
Bunch fresh mixed herbs
Ground nutmeg to taste
1–2 finely chopped onions

Salt and pepper
Olive oil for frying
10 sheets filo pastry
(see pages 177–8)

The bunch of herbs in Greece would include many mountain herbs and certainly some chopped dandelion. Highly flavoured herbs do improve the flavour of the pie and it will be more interesting if you can get them.

Wash the spinach, you can sprinkle it with pepper and salt and leave for an hour as in previous recipe, and then cook it in a pan without adding any more liquid than that which adheres to its leaves. Add the herbs, finely chopped, salt and pepper and cook the spinach until tender. In the meantime heat some olive oil and fry the onions until soft and beginning to brown. Take the onions from the pan, stir them into the spinach and chop this mixture until everything is blended and smooth. Line a roasting tin with oil. Spread the top layer with the spinach, add remaining sheets, brushing each with oil, sprinkle the top layer with a little water and bake the pie at 190°C/375°F/Gas 5 until the pastry is a golden brown, about 40 minutes. If the pastry begins to brown too quickly cover it with paper or lower the heat.

Greek cooking

Stuffed Tomatoes I

Domates Yemistes I

8 large, firm tomatoes
100g (4oz) long-grain rice
225ml (8fl oz) olive oil
2 finely chopped onions
25g (1oz) currants
25g (1oz) pine nuts

2 tablespoons finely chopped
  fresh mint
2 tablespoons finely chopped
  fresh parsley
Salt and pepper to taste
Breadcrumbs

Only because it looks nicer, choose tomatoes of uniform size. Slice off the stem end of each and scoop out the pulp, core and seeds. Chop this finely and sprinkle the inside of the tomatoes with a little salt and pepper.

Heat the oil and fry the onions to a golden brown. Stir in the tomato pulp, the rice, mint, parsley, salt, pepper, currants and pine nuts. Simmer for 2 minutes, then add 300ml (½ pint) of water and continue to cook slowly until the rice begins to soften, about 7 minutes.

Pack this mixture into the empty tomato cases, but do not completely fill them as the rice will swell. Replace the sliced off tops and arrange the tomatoes in an oiled baking tin. Brush each tomato with oil and sprinkle with breadcrumbs. Bake at 190°C/375°F/Gas 5 for about 45 minutes. Serve hot or cold, although cold is more usual in Greece.

Instead of first frying the stuffing, you can mix the chopped tomato pulp with the remaining ingredients in their raw state. This produces a slightly less rich dish.

Stuffed Tomatoes II

Domates Yemistes II

About 12 firm tomatoes
2–3 large chopped onions
275g (10oz) long-grain rice
4–5 cloves chopped garlic
1 large cored and finely chopped
  pepper
Handful chopped fresh parsley

1 tablespoon chopped fresh mint
1 tablespoon chopped currants
1 tablespoon pine nuts
225ml (8fl oz) olive oil
Salt and pepper
25g (1oz) tomato purée

Carefully cut round the upper part of the tomatoes at the stalk end. Remove the tops but keep these to use later as a lid. Scoop out the core and the pulp. Put the hollowed out tomatoes in a shallow baking dish, sprinkle with salt and leave until the filling is ready.

Chop the core into minute pieces and mix with the pulp. Put the chopped onions into a pan, add water to cover, bring to the boil and cook for 3 minutes. Drain off the water, add half the olive oil and simmer the onions. Add the tomato pulp and just cover with hot water. Bring to the boil, add the garlic, parsley, pepper, mint, seasoning, currants, pine nuts and finally the rice. Blend well and remove from the heat, the rice has not even begun to cook at this stage and the mixture should be comparatively loose. Fill some of this into each of the hollowed out tomatoes and put back the 'lids'. Put the remaining olive oil into the pan, add the tomato purée, diluted with enough water to make a thin gravy, and pour this over the tomatoes. Bake at 190°C/375°F/Gas 5 until the tomatoes are tender and the rice has cooked, roughly about 40 minutes.

Greek cooking

Tomatoes Stuffed with Minced Meat

Domates Yemistes Me Kima

Slice off the stalk end and scoop out the pulp from as many large and firm tomatoes as you require, they should, if possible, be of uniform size. Chop the pulp and core. Heat some olive oil and lightly fry some minced onion until brown, add a good quantity of raw minced beef or lamb, brown this, then add the tomato pulp, salt, pepper and chopped fresh parsley. Stir this mixture together, fry it for a few minutes and almost fill the empty tomato cases. Sprinkle the open tops with breadcrumbs. Put into a shallow baking tin, add enough hot water to prevent burning and bake at 190°C/375°F/Gas 5 until the tomatoes are soft.

Aubergines, peppers, onions and courgettes can all be stuffed and baked in the same manner.

For such recipes it is not too easy to give fixed quantities, since it depends so much on the size of the vegetables to be stuffed and individual taste. I think the experienced cook can easily decide how much stuffing goes into a tomato, and there are other recipes in this section which can act as a guide.

Tomatoes Stuffed with Aubergine

Domates Yemistes Me Melitzanes

8–10 large, firm tomatoes
2 medium-sized aubergines
2 medium-sized minced onions
90ml (3fl oz) olive oil
100g (4oz) fine breadcrumbs
3 tablespoons finely chopped
  fresh parsley

Salt and pepper
75g (3oz) grated Cheddar cheese
2 beaten eggs
A little sugar

Cut off the tops of the tomatoes and scoop out the pulp. Sprinkle the insides with salt and a little sugar and arrange them in a baking dish.

Without peeling, cut the aubergines into very small pieces. Heat two thirds of the oil, add the onions and simmer until they have become a light brown. Add the tomato pulp with the core (chopped into small pieces) and simmer for 5 minutes, then add the chopped aubergine and cook this until it is soft. Add half of the breadcrumbs, parsley, salt and pepper, cook and stir for 2 or 3 minutes. Remove from the fire and cool a little. Add the Cheddar cheese and when this is completely blended into the mixture, stir in the 2 eggs. Do this briskly otherwise you might find yourself with a curdled omelette. Beat the mixture before putting it into the tomatoes. Sprinkle the open top with the remaining breadcrumbs and oil. Put into a baking pan with hot water and bake at 190°C/375°F/Gas 5 until the tomatoes are tender.

The tomatoes should be really large and, if possible, all of uniform size.

Greek cooking

Shrimp Stuffed Tomatoes

Domates Yemistes Me Yarithes

Drop as many tomatoes as required into boiling water and leave for a minute or so, then peel. Leave until cold, before cutting off the tops and carefully removing the pulp. Fill the empty cases with cooked peeled shrimps or prawns which have been mixed with salad cream or mayonnaise. Chill before serving.

The pulp should be saved and used either in a soup or sauce.

Butter Beans Cooked with Tomatoes and Onions

Fassolia Yiyandes Plaki

700g (1 1/2lb) dried butter beans
700g (1 1/2lb) chopped onions
2 chopped cloves garlic
700g (1 1/2lb) peeled and chopped
  fresh tomatoes
225ml (8fl oz) olive oil
1 teaspoon sugar
Salt and pepper
2 tablespoons finely chopped
  fresh mint

Soak the beans overnight and next morning cook them rapidly in water for 5 minutes. Drain, return them to the stove with fresh, salted water and leave to cook until they are tender. Thoroughly drain them, keep the water, and in this cook the chopped onions for 5 minutes. Now drain off the water from the onions and add a quarter of the olive oil and cook the onions in this until they begin to brown. Add the beans, the tomatoes, garlic, remaining oil, salt, pepper, sugar and mint and continue cooking very slowly for another 30 minutes.

Both the onions and the tomatoes should be very finely chopped. Instead of fresh tomatoes you can use tinned (but first rub them through a sieve), or thick tomato juice. The quantity of mint can be reduced to taste, or, if preferred, use fresh parsley.

Dried Beans Boiled with Vegetables

Fassolia Yahni

This recipe can be used with all types of dried beans.

700g (1½lb) dried butter beans
225ml (8fl oz) olive oil
1 heaped tablespoon tomato
  purée
1–2 chopped onions

4 medium-sized, coarsely
  chopped carrots
1 bunch chopped celery
Salt and pepper
Bicarbonate of soda

Soak the beans overnight. Next morning put them into a large saucepan with plenty of water. Cover and bring them to the boil. Cook quickly for 20 minutes. Then add a pinch of bicarbonate of soda and continue to cook rapidly for another 15 minutes. Drain them well, add the olive oil, tomato purée (diluted with a little water), the onions, carrots, celery, salt and pepper. Add hot water to cover and bring this once to the boil, reduce the heat and continue cooking until the beans are quite tender.

Greek cooking

Mixed Lentils and Noodles
(Rhodes)

Alverof (Faki Me Pasta)

450g (1lb) lentils
350g (12oz) noodles
1–2 large, finely chopped onions
Olive oil or butter for frying

2.3 litres (4 pints) cold water
Salt and pepper to taste
300ml (1/2 pint) boiling water

Put the lentils into a pan with the water, cover and bring to the boil over a quick heat. Reduce the heat to moderate and continue cooking until the lentils are just soft. Add the noodles, broken into squares, salt and pepper, then the boiling water. Continue cooking over a good heat until the noodles are tender, about 20 minutes.

While this is cooking, fry the onions in oil or butter until brown. Strain the lentils and noodles, turn out on to a large, heated platter and garnish with the fried onions.

This is sufficient for 6 to 8 people and should be served very hot.

Dried Cannellini Beans with Pork

Fassolia Me Hirino

Soak 450g (1lb) of dried cannellini beans overnight and next morning cook them rapidly in water for 5 minutes. Drain, return them to the stove with fresh, salted water and leave to cook until they are tender. Drain. (The water can always be used as a basis for a soup.)

Fry in a little butter or oil 450g (1lb) of pork fillet cut into cubes or slices, add 1 large, minced onion, tomato juice to cover, salt and pepper and cook until the meat is tender, adding from time to time a very little hot water. When the meat is tender, add the drained beans, blend well, continue to cook for another 10 minutes, then serve hot.

Chick-peas

Revithia Yahni

Soak 900g (2lb) of chick-peas overnight, or better still for 24 hours. Drain and put them into a towel and then rub back and forth until the skins of the chick-peas are rubbed off. Put the peas into a pan with plenty of water and cook for 4 hours. When they are soft, flavour with chopped garlic, quite a lot of chopped onion, tomatoes, fresh mint or parsley, salt and pepper. Cook gently for another 20 minutes, the heat should be low but the chick-peas must be boiling all the time. The best way to cook chick-peas is to have them on the side of a large coal - or coke-burning stove.

This would be considered rather in the nature of a Lenten dish, or a dish for a canteen or families with hearty appetites. Sometimes pieces of pork are added or garlic sausage, although this latter is more of a Spanish custom than Greek. 900g (2lb) of chick-peas makes a solid meal for 6 to 8 people.

Greek cooking

Rice and Pasta
Pilafi ke Pasta

Pilau

Pilafi

A basic recipe which can be adjusted to suit individual tastes. If you do not care for the flavour of tomato, omit the tomato paste.

450g (1lb) long-grain rice
1.2 litres (2 pints) vegetable stock
125ml (4fl oz) olive oil

1 tablespoon tomato paste
Salt and pepper to taste

Dilute the tomato paste with some of the vegetable stock. Heat the oil and add the rice. Stir and cook over a medium heat for 5 minutes, the rice becomes almost transparent. Add the stock to the pan but do it fairly slowly for when the stock touches the pan it causes an alarming, sizzling noise. Add salt and pepper, cover and cook over a slow heat for about 20 minutes. By this time all the liquid will have been absorbed and the rice will be tender but dry.

To help the drying process most Greek and Balkan cooks wrap the saucepan lid in flannel or a napkin and then clamp the lid on tightly. The cloth absorbs the steam rapidly, prevents further swelling of the rice and you can keep it in the pan longer.

Tomato Pilau

Pilafi Me Domates

450g (1lb) long-grain rice
1.2 litres (2 pints) vegetable stock
4 large, peeled and chopped
   tomatoes

2 tablespoons tomato paste
125ml (4fl oz) olive oil
Salt and pepper
1 teaspoon sugar (optional)

Heat the oil in a saucepan and fry the rice for 5 minutes. Add the tomatoes and simmer for 10 minutes. Dilute the tomato paste with the stock, add salt, pepper and sugar (if used) and pour this into the pan; bring to the boil, lower the heat and cover tightly. Cook for 10 minutes. Lower the heat to almost nothing and continue for another 30 minutes, preferably with the lid wrapped in a napkin.

Baked Rice Pilau (Greek-American)

Pilafi Tou Fournou

450g (1lb) long-grain rice
1.2 litres (2 pints) vegetable stock

Salt to taste

Thoroughly wash the rice and soak it in boiling water for 30 minutes. Drain and shake it dry. In the meantime bring the stock to boiling point in a casserole. Heat the oven to 230°F/450°F/Gas 8, stir the rice into the stock, add salt, cover and put the casserole into the oven. Lower to 190°C/375°F/Gas 5 and bake the rice for 15 minutes.

Remove the cover, wrap it in a cloth and replace it, then turn off the heat and leave the casserole in the oven for 30 minutes. Serve the pilau either in the casserole or turn it out on to a hot platter. If all the liquid has been absorbed, as it should be, it will turn out in the shape of the casserole. Garnish it with anything you like, fish, meat or chicken or baked tomatoes. Or you can mix all kinds of things such as chicken livers, strips of meat or chicken, fresh parsley or other herbs with the rice while it is cooking.

Greek cooking

Two To One Pilau

Dyo-m' Ena Pilafi

225g (8oz) long-grain rice   Butter
450ml (3/4 pint) water

Bring the water to the boil, add the rice and cook until tender, about 15 minutes. Cover the pan with a napkin to absorb any remaining water and also to prevent any further swelling of the rice. Heat the butter until it bubbles, then pour this into the rice. Run a fork lightly through the grains to let the butter penetrate. Serve at once.

    Tomatoes or tomato juice can be added but the quantity of liquid must always be just 450ml (3/4 pint).

    Enough for 2 people. Instead of water a light vegetable stock may be used which, of course, improves the flavour of the pilau.

Pilau with Mussels

Mythia Pilafi

225g (8oz) fresh mussels
450g (1lb) long-grain rice
1.2 litres (2 pints) water
1 finely chopped onion

50ml (2fl oz) olive oil
150ml (1/4 pint) dry white wine
Salt and pepper

Wash the mussels thoroughly in several waters, scrubbing or scraping their shells. Heat the oil, add the onion and fry it until it begins to brown. Add the mussels, stir once or twice and leave until the mussels begin to open, then add the wine, water, salt and pepper. Bring the liquid to the boil, lower the heat, then cook the mussels gently for 10 minutes. By this time the mussels should be quite open, if they are not, then they are not fresh. With a perforated spoon take the mussels from the pan, put aside, and throw the rice into the mussel stock. Let this boil for 15 minutes while you deal with the mussels. Open the shells, discard these, and remove the edible flesh, discarding the dark part. Return the mussels to the pan just 5 minutes before the rice is ready. As soon as the rice is tender, take the pan from the fire, cover it with a napkin, clamp on the lid, and put the saucepan on the side of the stove. Leave for 20 minutes, by which time all the moisture in the rice will have been absorbed.

Greek cooking

Shrimp Pilau

Garithes Pilafi

225g (8oz) frozen peeled prawns
  or shrimps, thawed
125ml (4fl oz) olive oil
2 finely chopped onions

350g (12oz) long-grain rice
Salt and pepper
Pinch marjoram

Heat the olive oil in a heavy saucepan and lightly fry the onions, until soft but not brown. Add the rice and cook for 5 minutes or until the rice becomes almost transparent. Add the shrimp water, which must be boiling. Bring the rice and the water to the boil, add salt, pepper and marjoram to taste, lower the heat, add the prawns or shrimps, cover tightly (wrap the lid in a cloth for better steam absorption) and cook until the rice is tender. Leave for 20 minutes, still covered, on the side of the stove.

Spaghetti with a Meat Sauce

Spagheto Me Kima Saltsa

450g (1lb) spaghetti
450g (1lb) minced beef or lamb
2 finely chopped onions
2–3 chopped cloves garlic
1–2 bay leaves
2 tablespoons tomato paste

4–6 peeled and chopped
  tomatoes
1/2 teaspoon ground cinnamon
3 tablespoons olive oil
Salt and pepper
Water

A recipe from Rhodes but popular throughout Greece.

Heat the pan and sauté the meat for 5 minutes, frequently shaking the pan. Add the oil, when this is hot add the onions, garlic and tomatoes. Simmer for about 10 minutes. Add the tomato paste diluted with 225ml (8fl oz) of water, salt, pepper, cinnamon and bay leaves, stir well and bring to the boil. Reduce the heat to very low and continue to cook gently for 30 minutes or until the meat is quite tender and the onions and tomatoes reduced to a thick sauce.

While this is cooking, bring a saucepan of salted water to the boil, gradually add the spaghetti, letting the water cook rapidly all the while. Cook the spaghetti quickly for 15 minutes. Drain and shake dry, you can pour a little olive oil over it if you like, arrange on a very hot platter, slightly indent the middle, then pour the meat and Tomato Sauce into the hollow. Serve at once.

Noodles with Lentils *(Rhodes)*

Pasta Ke Faki

Another recipe with a strong Italian influence.

Noodles	Pinch salt
Plain flour, about 350g (12oz)	Water

Mix the flour, salt and water to a dough and knead until pliable. Roll out very thinly, it is better to use a very thin roller and let the pastry wind itself around this as you roll. If you have only the usual rolling pin, then continue rolling until the dough is thin. Cut it into noodle shapes, they should be roughly 1cm (1/2in) wide by 5cm (2in) long.

450g (1lb) lentils	Salt and pepper
1 finely chopped onion	Butter

Cook the lentils until soft in plenty of water. Add the noodles, salt and pepper and continue to cook until these are tender, about 10 minutes should be long enough. Chop and brown the onion in butter. Drain the lentils and noodles, turn on to a dish and garnish with the fried onion.

Commercially made noodles or tagliatelle may also be used.

Greek cooking

Sauces
Saltses

Greek sauces are quite individual and there are not many of them. But it was the Greeks who invented sauces. Orion, who is one of the seven sages of the culinary arts, invented the white sauce, while Lampriades, another culinary sage, introduced the brown sauce. There was yet another sauce of great antiquity and fame, a fish sauce invented by the poet Menander, but, although its fame has come down through some twenty centuries of cooking, the recipe has been lost.

But Greeks still feel strongly on the question of sauces. Xenophon, the cook of a Greek friend of mine, was in search of a job because his master had left Athens. He was offered one in a good, even exclusive, restaurant, but he refused. Asked the reason for his refusal he replied, 'Working in a restaurant would ruin my sauces, they even put flour in a mayonnaise.' Now he is happy working for some French archaeologists who simply adore his sauces.

Béchamel Sauce

Saltsa Béchamel

Used in a great number of Greek recipes, it is simply white sauce with a slight difference.

50g (2oz) butter
50–75g (2–3oz) plain flour
900ml (1 1/2 pints) milk

Salt and pepper to taste
Good pinch ground nutmeg

Scald the milk. Heat the butter in a saucepan and gradually work in the flour until smooth. Slowly add the milk, stirring it all the while, add the nutmeg, salt and pepper and cook very slowly until the sauce is thick and there is no odour of flour. It is better to cook for 15 or 20 minutes, stirring all the while.

Egg and Lemon Sauce

Saltsa Avgolemono

This extremely good sauce is the national sauce of Greece. It is simply egg and lemon beaten together and stirred into whatever dish requires it. It is frequently used for flavouring soups, and just as often with meat, fish, vegetable and poultry dishes. All that is essential is that the dish which is to be flavoured with this sauce has some liquid, from which to take 2 or 3 tablespoons. This is stirred into the egg and lemon and then the sauce goes into the pan.

4 egg yolks
4 tablespoons lemon juice

2–3 tablespoons hot broth
or vegetable stock

Beat the egg yolks until fluffy and light, then slowly add the lemon juice, beating all the while. Gradually add 2 or 3 tablespoons of the liquid from the dish you have prepared. Then the sauce is stirred into the dish you are making. Leave for 5 minutes on the side of the stove, above all do not let the sauce boil, and keep the pan covered.

Instead of 4 egg yolks you can use 2 or 3 whole eggs.

Greek cooking

Garlic Sauce with Potatoes

Skorthalia Me Patates

Skorthalia or garlic sauce is a favourite of the Greeks and is eaten with many types of meat, fish and vegetable dishes although the most important marriage is *skorthalia* with salt fish. There are several ways of making it, with potatoes, with nuts, with breadcrumbs or with flour.

6 medium-sized potatoes	175ml (6fl oz) olive oil
4–6 cloves garlic	Strained juice 2 lemons
1 teaspoon salt	

Wash the potatoes and boil them in their skins until soft. Peel them as soon as they are cool enough to handle and mash. Crush the garlic with the salt (do this while the potatoes are cooking), mix with the mashed potatoes and continue to pound until these ingredients are blended and the mixture is smooth. Gradually add the olive oil drop by drop, alternating with the lemon juice, stirring all the while until you have a thick cream. When you are ready to serve the sauce you can, if you like, dilute it just a little either with fish or meat stock.

Garlic Sauce with Breadcrumbs

Skorthalia Me Yaletta

225g (8oz) soft breadcrumbs	Juice 1 lemon
175ml (6fl oz) olive oil	Salt to taste
6–8 cloves garlic	

Crush the garlic to a paste with about 1 teaspoon of salt. Add the breadcrumbs and beat until the breadcrumbs and garlic are mixed like a paste. Gradually add the olive oil and lemon juice, alternately until you have a sauce of the same consistency as mayonnaise.

A similar sauce can be made with a flour and water paste, using the same quantity of plain flour, and some Greeks consider this to be much lighter.

Garlic Sauce with Almonds

Skorthalia Me Amygthala

1 medium-sized potato
175g (6oz) blanched and
  ground almonds
6–8 cloves garlic

Juice 1 lemon
1 teaspoon salt
175ml (6fl oz) olive oil

Cook the potato until soft (preferably in its skin) and, while it is cooking, crush the garlic and salt until smooth. Add the almonds and mix until a smooth paste is formed. By this time the potato will be cooked. Peel this and mash it until smooth, then add it to the paste. When well-blended, add the olive oil and lemon juice, drop by drop until you have a thick sauce, stiff enough to hold its shape.

Garlic and Egg Sauce
(Istanbul-Greek)

Skorthalia Me Avgo

4 cloves garlic
1 teaspoon salt
2 egg yolks

Olive oil
Lemon juice or wine vinegar

Crush the garlic with the salt, beat in the 2 egg yolks and then gradually add, drop by drop, enough olive oil to make a sauce of mayonnaise consistency. Loosen with either lemon juice or wine vinegar.

Greek cooking

Pistachio Sauce

Skorthalia Me Fystikia

100g (4oz) pistachio nuts
50g (2oz) soft white bread
4 cloves garlic

Olive oil
Lemon juice or wine vinegar

Grind the nuts (peeled, of course) in a blender or food processor with the garlic until the mixture is smooth. Soak the bread in water and squeeze it dry. Mix with the nuts and work the mixture till smooth. Gradually add enough olive oil to make a thick sauce, then loosen it with either lemon juice or wine vinegar.

Lemon and Mustard Sauce

Saltsa Moustartha

Juice 2 lemons
Double this quantity olive oil
Salt and pepper to taste

1 teaspoon dried English mustard
2 chopped cloves garlic
Chopped fresh parsley

Put the lemon juice, well strained, into a bowl and gradually add double the quantity of olive oil, salt, pepper, mustard and garlic. Stir together until blended, then strain. Serve sprinkled lightly with finely chopped fresh parsley.

Mayonnaise Sauce

Saltsa Mayioneza

There are several ways of making mayonnaise sauce. This is a typical Greek method of which Xenophon would not approve.

225ml (8fl oz) olive oil
225ml (8fl oz) good quality vinegar
1 tablespoon dry English mustard
1/2 teaspoon salt

2 tablespoons lemon juice
1 egg yolk
25g (1oz) plain flour

Stir the flour in a bowl and mix with a little water to a paste. Add mustard, salt and egg yolk. When blended, add a few drops of vinegar and a few drops more of water. Add the oil, a little at a time, stirring briskly all the while. When the mixture is quite thick, add the lemon juice and the remaining ingredients and stir until smooth. If it is a little too stiff, cautiously add a little more lemon juice.

Tomato Sauce I

Saltsa Domates I

700g (11/2lb) tomatoes
300ml (1/2 pint) water
1 teaspoon sugar

1 teaspoon cornflour
25g (1oz) butter
Salt and pepper

Peel the tomatoes (dip them into boiling water first to make this operation easier). Slice them thickly and put into a pan, without adding any liquid, and simmer gently until they begin to soften. Add remaining ingredients and continue cooking until the tomatoes are soft. Rub through a strainer and use as required.

Sometimes chopped onion is added. It is first lightly fried in butter until soft and put in the pan at the same time as the cornflour, etc.

This is a sauce for immediate use. It is easier to mix the cornflour with water to a paste before using it.

Greek cooking

Tomato Sauce II

Saltsa Domates II

1.4kg (3lb) tomatoes
1 small, chopped onion
1 finely chopped carrot
1 finely chopped stick celery
Chopped garlic to taste

Salt and pepper
1 teaspoon sugar
25g (1oz) plain flour
25g (1oz) butter

Wash the tomatoes and cook them with the vegetables, garlic and seasoning until very soft. Rub through a sieve. Heat the butter, stir in the flour and cook for a minute or so. Add the strained Tomato Sauce and the sugar, stirring all the while, and cook slowly until the sauce is thick.

For immediate use but will keep for a while, especially if stored in a refrigerator. The above quantity will make about 1.2 litres (2 pints) of sauce, much depends on the juiciness of the tomatoes.

Tomato Sauce III

Saltsa Domates III

5.4kg (12lb) tomatoes
900g (2lb) onions
1–2 chopped cloves garlic
1 grated nutmeg
1 tablespoon ground ginger

6 tablespoons salt
1 teaspoon pepper
300ml (1/2 pint) vinegar
100g (4oz) sugar

Chop the tomatoes and onions coarsely and put into a large saucepan with the garlic, nutmeg, ginger, salt and pepper, and cook very slowly until the tomatoes are soft, cook for at least 2 hours. Rub this through a sieve and leave until cool. Add the vinegar and sugar, return the sauce to the pan, and continue to cook until the sauce is thick. Cool and pour into bottles.

Salad Dressing or Sauce

Ladoxitho

175ml (6fl oz) olive oil
50ml (2fl oz) vinegar

1/4 teaspoon dry English mustard
Pinch salt and pepper

Put these ingredients into a jar, seal and shake until blended. Chill before serving.

Salads
Salates

When the Greeks talk of salads they do not mean a mixture of lettuce, cucumber, beetroot and spring onions, garnished with a mayonnaise sauce. Generally vegetables used for salads are simply dressed with olive oil, not always by any means to the foreigners' taste. Greek salads are made from a large choice of vegetables, including many wild varieties, or herbs from the mountains. These are all prepared in the manner of spinach salad (see page 175). Especially popular are dandelion leaves, a salad so nicely rendered in Zonar's menu as 'tandel lion'. Dandelion is credited with the curing of many ills, particularly those of the stomach. Also a salad can be what we would call a purée, such as aubergine or *taramo* salad; or dried beans cooked and served in a dressing; or beetroot, cooked and sliced, served with any of the *skorthalia* or garlic sauces.

Fish Roe Salad (Botargo)

Avgotaraho: Taramosalata

According to the *Oxford Dictionary* botargo is a relish of mullet or cod roe. The Greek word comes from *tarihkion*, which means pickled or pickle. Sometimes *avgotaraho* goes under the name of 'red caviare'. It has a unique flavour, is as thick as caramel, extremely rich, and adheres somewhat to the teeth and the roof of the mouth. It is not known much in Britain, although Samuel Pepys records on 6 June 1661, 'We stayed talking and singing and drinking great draughts of claret, and eating botargo and bread-and-butter till twelve at night.' As he does not mention it with any kind of explanation it must have been well known, like so many other items of diet which are now considered exotic. Botargo in those days was called, 'a sausage made from the eggs and the blood of the mullet'.

The method of collecting the eggs from the grey mullet is interesting. The collecting grounds in Greece (there are others in Turkey and in some Arab countries as well) are called *tzenios* and the area around is cleared of all seaweed, which is replaced by an ingenious system of 'cane weirs'. In August, when the female grey mullet is ready to spawn and is looking for a quiet spawning ground, she is tricked into the false weirs and at once speared with amazing dexterity by fishermen lying in wait for her in flat-bottomed boats. The roe, which is in two sections, is immediately removed from the belly, cleaned of all its membranes, soaked in brine for several hours, and then put into the sun to dry. The dried roe can be eaten at once, but it is generally covered with a thick coating of beeswax in order to preserve it. This is, of course, removed for eating. In this stage the roe is called 'red caviare' and is sliced and eaten as an appetizer. I find it irresistible and can eat far too much of it.

To make taramasalata you put into a mixing bowl as much roe as will be required, say about 100g (4oz), and mix it with an equal quantity of bread, which has been soaked in water, squeezed dry and then pounded until smooth. When the roe and the bread are really well blended, gradually add olive oil until the mixture has the consistency of a soft, but not too soft, purée. Then add just enough lemon juice to loosen it slightly. Some people add a minute quantity of water to make the purée even lighter and creamier, others an egg yolk, previously well beaten. Then again the quantity of bread can be reduced. It should be served as an appetizer. In Britain it can be

Greek cooking

served as an unusual but delicious prelude to a small dinner, or a large one for that matter. Failing grey mullet roe quite a good salad can be made with cod's roe but this will not, of course, have the same flavour.

Incidentally, when I talk of red caviare I do not mean the loose variety. Botargo is definitely dried and firmly pressed.

Aubergine Salad (or Purée)

Melitzanosalata

2 aubergines, fairly large	Salt and pepper to taste
1 medium-sized grated onion	90ml (3fl oz) olive oil
1 tablespoon chopped fresh parsley	Juice half a lemon or vinegar
1 chopped clove garlic	

Remove the green ends and grill the aubergines until the skins turn brown and begin to break. (This is best done over a charcoal fire.) As soon as you can handle the aubergines rip off all the skin and pound the flesh in a bowl. Add the onion and garlic and continue to pound until the mixture is smooth, adding salt and pepper as you work, Greeks add rather more salt than we are apt to. When the mixture is reasonably smooth, add the olive oil gradually until it is like a stiff mayonnaise. Beat in the parsley and the lemon juice or vinegar. Serve cold.

The nicest way to eat this and other similar purées is to scoop it up with chunks of soft, brown bread.

White Beans in Oil

Fassolia Salata

By this I mean the large, dried beans called butter beans in Britain or giant beans by the Greeks.

Cook the beans in the usual manner and when they are drained but still warm coat them with olive oil, sprinkle lightly with grated onion and a little chopped fresh parsley. Serve cold.

Cucumber and Yoghurt Salad

Tzatziki

600ml (1 pint) yoghurt
1 chopped clove garlic
1 small grated cucumber

1 tablespoon olive oil
1 tablespoon vinegar
Salt

Beat the yoghurt, add the remaining ingredients and then chill. In Macedonian Greece *tzatziki* is served as a soup.

Green Bean Salad

Salata Fassolakia

You should use either very young runner beans for this salad or French beans, small enough to leave whole, with only the ends trimmed. With beans which are long but tender, break them into halves. Cook them in just enough boiling water to cover with a little soda added, and salt and pepper. When they are tender, pour away any remaining water and replace it with enough olive oil to coat each bean. Leave until cool, then add about 2 tablespoons of lemon juice, and some finely chopped garlic. Stir with a wooden spoon and serve when really very cold.

Very good also with a garlic sauce.

Spinach Salad

Spanaki Salata

Wash as much spinach as required, removing all coarse leaves and thick stalks. Cook it in a saucepan without adding water for 15 minutes. Drain it thoroughly and arrange in a salad bowl. Add an olive oil and lemon dressing, salt and pepper, stir it round and round until all the spinach is well covered with the dressing, and serve either hot or cold, the latter is preferable.

Greek cooking

Pastries, Cakes and Sweet Dishes
Ylyka

Many Greek pastries and sweet dishes are of ancient origin and they are quite different from those we are used to eating in Britain, or for that matter, in France. Generally speaking, Greeks do not finish a meal with a sweet dish: when they eat sweets it is for a special occasion, such as a wedding, or a name giving ceremony and, of course, on the many days of festival.

So in this way Greeks do eat large quantities of sweet dishes in some form or other. And I think it is fair to say that never have I seen quite so many sweet or pastry shops as in Athens , except perhaps in Istanbul. Shop after shop is filled with honey-flavoured sweet pastries, with row after row of cakes and pastries wrapped in gold, silver or scarlet paper, looking very luscious and tempting.

I remember one day I was taken by a Greek friend to Lutosi, which is near Corinth, simply to eat pastries. There were all varieties of *baklava* and *kataifi*, one variety I remember was called Laïs, after a well-known courtesan of that name whose love was so sweet. There was *melogarida*, which is honey and walnuts pressed together to such a sticky, hard mass that it becomes almost like a wafer biscuit, and is excellent. I ate *karithopita*, or Athenian walnut cake, and chocolate cake, marzipan and fruit cake, never have I eaten so many cakes in one session. And then my charming hosts went to the great glass counters and, in consultation with one of the girl assistants, picked me out a variety of their choicest silver and gold wrapped pastries. Fortunately the wrapped pastries were made to last, I was not expected to have another pastry-eating session that day.

Almost all Greek pastries seem to be soaked in honey, and seem at first glance to be difficult to prepare. If you are able to buy Greek filo pastry, nothing could be easier than making a *baklava* pastry and for a change it is really to be recommended. Oddly enough, sweet though this pastry is, I do suggest you try it with Devonshire cream. This is not Greek taste, but in Istanbul we used to eat all these honey-soaked pastries with a portion of *kaimak*, which is a thick cream so firm that it can be cut into slices.

The halvah recipe I have given is not the same halvah that we buy in supermarkets or specialist shops or when travelling in the Middle East. Almost all sweet dishes made with semolina and nuts become halvah, right through to India. The halvah of the shops is a sticky, almost crisp textured sweet, heavily flavoured with sesame, available only in winter since it melts easily. It is absolutely delicious, but like so many good things, figure shattering.

Turkish delight or *loukoum*, although available in Greek shops, is really Turkish, the secret of its preparation still being in the hands of one Istanbul family. Other firms make it, but it is not quite the same. Cypriot Greeks also prepare *loukoum*. I have not mentioned ice-cream in this section, which may seem to some students of Greece rather odd, as Athens is famous for its ice-creams. Most of the Greek ice-cream gets its richness from the ewe's milk with which it is made and even if I gave recipes the flavour would not be quite the same. But ice-cream has always seemed to me to be better throughout the Balkans than the ice-cream we serve in Britain, probably because in our summers we do not have the violent urge to cool ourselves with ice-cream. In the Balkans and Greece one does.

Greek Pastry I

Phyllo

Filo is a plain, paper-thin pastry used in most Greek pastries and pies, whether savoury or sweet, and requires an expert to make it properly. It is bought by the pound in Greece (and in the Balkan countries as well as in the Middle East) in shops which sell only filo and *kataifi* pastry.

The dough for making filo is simple enough, flour and water mixed to a stiff paste. From this pieces are broken and rolled into balls roughly the size of a tennis ball. At this stage an expert must take over. First he tosses a ball of dough back and forth between his large, capable hands, then up and down and along his brawny arms, until it becomes like a thin circle of parchment paper. Then it is twirled round and round in the air until it becomes even larger and thinner, a fascinating operation to watch, as good as any juggler's act. After this the round of pastry is thrown with unerring aim on to a specially constructed round metal disc, about the size of a small table in diameter, and it is stretched and stretched and stretched until the almost agonized watcher feels it must break, that this stretching cannot go on any longer, but it does. Finally, when everyone is satisfied that the pastry has reached the absolute limit of its endurance, it is cut into sizes suitable for making the pies and pastries to which the people of Greece are accustomed.

continued

Greek cooking

Home-made filo cannot compete with the professional variety, but even so a passable imitation is possible. You need to mix as much plain flour, baking powder and water as required to a stiff dough. The quantity of baking powder to flour is 2 teaspoons to every 900g (2lb) of flour. Knead it as much as you are able and set it aside for 2 hours. Then, like the professionals, break off pieces of about tennis ball size and roll these out until the pastry is very thin. It can be done; I have done it myself and made a passable imitation of Greek pies. I use a thin rolling pin and when the pastry is really thin I roll it round the pin and roll it back and forth until the pastry becomes, well, not quite paper thin, but very thin.

When using home-made filo use less than half the quantity of pastry called for in the recipe.

Greek Pastry II

Kataifi

This, like filo, is made by professional pastry makers. The dough, however, is much thinner and squeezed through a tin with a perforated bottom straight on to the metal disc which, however, is hot. The pastry is not cooked on the disc but merely set into long thin strands which look very like strands of spaghetti. It is sold in the same kind of shops which sell filo.

Almond Stuffed Rolls

Floyeres

6 sheets filo pastry
100g (4oz) almonds or walnuts
50g (2oz) sugar

1 beaten egg
Fresh butter, slightly melted

Syrup

225g (8oz) sugar
1 pint water

1 teaspoon lemon juice
1 small piece cinnamon

Six sheets of filo pastry will make 24 rolls.

Blanch the nuts and either grind or crush them. Mix with the egg and sugar. This makes the filling.

Cut each sheet of filo into 4 strips and brush each strip with butter. Put a heaped teaspoonful of the filling on to one end of each strip of filo and roll up each in the manner of a Swiss roll. Arrange these on a greased baking sheet lined with greaseproof paper and bake at 190°C/375°F/Gas 5 until a golden brown, about 25 minutes.

Put the syrup ingredients into a shallow pan and bring to the boil, then simmer until the syrup is of a medium thickness. As soon as the turnovers are ready, take them from the oven and put 2 or 3 into a perforated spoon and dip them into the still simmering syrup. Do this once or twice then put the rolls on to a large platter. When all the rolls have been dipped in the syrup leave them until cold. *Floyeres* will keep for several days, at least they will in theory, but in practice they usually disappear rapidly, for in Greece they are very popular.

Pastry Filled with Walnuts and Steeped in Syrup

Baklava

A sweet, nut-filled pastry which the traveller begins to discover as soon as he arrives in the Balkans. Whether it was invented by the Greeks or the Turks (or the Russians) is always a matter of argument between Hellenophiles and Turcophiles.

575g (1¼lb) filo pastry
  (about 25 to 30 sheets)
350g (¾lb) blanched
  and chopped walnuts

450g (1lb) unsalted butter, melted
1 tablespoon ground cinnamon
  (or to taste)

Syrup

450g (1lb) jar of clear honey
225g (8oz) sugar

900ml (1½ pints) warm water
1 teaspoon lemon juice

For filo pastry see pages 177–8.

Mix the walnuts with the cinnamon. Grease a baking sheet to match the size of your sheets of pastry, and line it with 1 sheet of pastry. Brush this

continued

lightly with melted butter. Add another sheet, butter this and sprinkle lightly with the cinnamoned walnuts. Add 2 more pastry sheets brushed only with butter, then another with butter and walnuts, and repeat this operation until you have about 8 or 10 pastry sheets left. By this time all the walnuts should be finished. Add the last sheets brushed with butter. Dip a sharp knife into boiling water and score through the first 4 sheets making squares of a serving size. Sprinkle the top sheet of pastry with water (this is to prevent it from curling upwards). Bake the *baklava* at 190°C/375°F/Gas 5 for about 1 1/2 hours. Let it cool before adding the syrup.

While the *baklava* is baking make the syrup. Boil all the syrup ingredients together until the mixture is syrupy but not too thick. While it is still boiling pour it slowly over the cooled *baklava*. Cool again before seeing, by which time most of the syrup should be absorbed.

There are some cooks who add a piece of cinnamon to the syrup, others who sprinkle each sheet of pastry with sugar, but this makes the *baklava* even sweeter than it is already.

Instead of squares the top sheets of pastry can be scored into diamond, oval or oblong shapes.

Sweet Pastry Rolls

Kataifi

Professionally made *kataifi* rolls look rather like stuffed Shredded Wheat, but here the resemblance ends. Nonprofessional cooks make their *kataifi* in the manner described below, the flavour is the same, they just do not look quite so elegant.

Filling

350g (12oz) blanched
  and chopped walnuts
175g (6oz) melted butter

100g (4oz) sugar
1/2 teaspoon ground cinnamon

Syrup

450g (1lb) sugar
100ml (1 1/2 pints) water

Orange or lemon rind
1 teaspoon lemon juice

There are two ways of preparing *kataifi*. Correctly and more professionally you spread out enough of the *kataifi* pastry in your left hand to cover it, sprinkle it with filling and then gently close the 2 ends, pressing them artfully together. Less professional but simpler is to lay half the *kataifi* pastry in the bottom of a shallow baking tin, spread this with walnuts, sugar and cinnamon, add half the butter and then cover with the remaining *kataifi*. Pour the remaining butter over the top layer of *kataifi* and bake at 190°C/375°F/Gas 5 for about 1½ hours. Boil the syrup ingredients together until you have a medium-thick syrup and pour this over the *kataifi* while it is still hot. Cover with a napkin so that the steam will be absorbed and the surface becomes soft. Cool and cut into squares or diamonds to serve.

Actually making *kataifi* is not difficult but for some mysterious reason, just as one's cherished pastry recipes sometimes fail, so do the *kataifi* rolls. Even cooks who normally can make perfect *kataifi* sometimes find they are too hard and cannot be broken, or sometimes the syrup goes wrong and they become too soggy. But when they are good, they are very, very good.

Vanilla Cream Pie

Galatoboureko

20 sheets filo pastry   175g (6oz) melted butter

Filling

2.3 litres (4 pints) milk   175g (6oz) semolina
450g (1lb) sugar   A few strips lemon peel
6 eggs   Vanilla flavouring to taste

Syrup

450g (1lb) sugar   1 teaspoon lemon juice
1.2 litres (2 pints) water   A little lemon peel

Heat the milk to scalding point and take from the heat. Beat the eggs with the sugar until thick and creamy, add vanilla flavouring and lemon peel, stir well, then gradually add the semolina, beating all the time. Slowly add the scalded milk and then put the mixture back into the saucepan. Cook over a

continued

low heat until the mixture thickens, stirring all the time. Take the pan from the heat and continue stirring or beating until the mixture is quite cool.

Grease a shallow baking tin somewhat smaller than your sheets of pastry and line it with 1 sheet of pastry, the edge of the pastry should come up above the top of the tin. Add the semolina-cream and turn back the edges of the pastry over the cream to keep this from oozing out. Cover with remaining sheets of pastry, each spread with melted butter. With a sharp knife trace or score the first 4 sheets of pastry into serving sections, either in squares or diamonds, sprinkle the top layer with water and bake at 190°C/375°F/Gas 5 for about 1½ hours.

Boil the syrup ingredients to a medium-thick syrup and pour this over the pie when you take it from the oven, it is better to do this gradually. Cool before serving.

Greeks prefer to use vanilla crystals for flavouring rather than essence. I prefer to use vanilla bean but it is a matter for personal preference.

Enough for about 12 people.

Failing filo pastry the filling is excellent when used in the same way as in a custard-cream pie.

Greek Shortbread

Kourabiethes

Kourabiethes, traditionally, are made both for the New Year celebrations and for Christmas. It is claimed that their history can be traced back to the days of St John Chrysostom who is said to have mentioned *kourabiethes* during one of his sermons. Each shortbread or *kourabiethes* should be stuck with one clove to represent the Three Wise Men who brought spices to the Christ Child.

 Kourabiethes, like Christmas puddings or mince pies, must be made with loving care and cooks like to specialize in them. One Greek friend of mine refuses to eat them anywhere but in her mother's home. She says the quality and flavour depends absolutely on the creaming of the butter and this should be done with the hand and fingers for at least 30 minutes. She remembers her mother sitting happily in their large kitchen, her hands deep in creamy butter, beating and beating, and, she adds, her mother's *kourabiethes* were the best in the whole of Greece. This is her mother's recipe, but how much you beat will depend on time, modern conditions and patience. I think a modern rotary mixer can bring the butter to the creaminess desired, although my friend thinks not.

900g (2lb) plain flour
450g (1lb) unsalted butter
175g (6oz) sugar
1 teaspoon baking powder
1 tablespoon ouzo (see pages 235–6)

1 teaspoon vanilla essence
2 egg yolks
Rosewater
Icing sugar
Cloves

Sift the flour with the baking powder. Cream the butter with the sugar and then add the ouzo and the vanilla, the egg yolks and gradually enough flour to make a soft but firm dough. If there is not enough liquid, add either some more ouzo or another egg yolk, if you have made the dough too loose, then add more flour. Break off small pieces, pat these into biscuit shapes and place on a floured baking sheet. Insert a clove into each shortbread and bake at 190°C/375°F/Gas 5 for about 20 minutes, until they are cooked through but not browned. Take from the oven and while still hot sprinkle with icing sugar and then rosewater. Do this once more, then cool. *Kourabiethes* will stay fresh for 2 or 3 weeks.

Greek cooking

Shortbread with Almonds

Kourabiethes Me Amygthalo

Prepare as in the preceding recipe but add 50g (2oz) of blanched and chopped almonds and 2 or 3 toasted and chopped almonds.

Almond Pears

Amygthalota

450g (1lb) blanched almonds
225g (8oz) castor sugar
3 egg whites
75g (3oz) soft breadcrumbs
Vanilla essence to taste

Orange flower water
Icing sugar
Butter
Cloves

Mix the almonds with 25g (1oz) of sugar and grind them until very fine. Add remaining sugar, vanilla essence, egg whites and the breadcrumbs. Knead this mixture to a dough, then break off small pieces. Shape these into 'pears' and at the end of each insert 1 clove to represent the stalk. Arrange on a baking sheet lined with greaseproof paper and bake for 15 minutes at 190°C/375°F/Gas 5. When the almond pears are cool, dip them quickly into orange flower water and then lightly coat with icing sugar.

You can, of course, use ground almonds.

The cooks of the island of Hydra, just off the mainland, are known for their particular version of almond pears and they are worth asking for.

Athenian Walnut Cake

Karithopita Athinaiki

700g (1 1/2lb) plain flour
700g (1 1/2lb) shelled walnuts
275g (10oz) sugar
100g (4oz) butter

8 eggs
2 teaspoons cinnamon
2 teaspoons baking powder

Syrup

300g (12oz) sugar
600ml (1 pint) water

150–300ml (1/4–1/2 pint) brandy
(optional)

Coarsely grind the walnuts and put aside 2 tablespoons. Separate the egg yolks from the whites and beat the latter until stiff. Beat the butter and sugar together until creamy, add the egg yolks one by one, beating all the while. Add half the beaten egg white and the cinnamon. Still beating, gradually add the flour, baking powder and the walnuts. When all this is blended, fold in the remaining egg white. Turn the mixture into a greased cake tin, lined with greaseproof paper, measuring 30 x 23 x 5cm (12 x 9 x 2in). Sprinkle with the remaining walnuts and bake at 190°C/375°F/Gas 5 for about 30 or 40 minutes.

While the cake is baking make a syrup by boiling the sugar and water together until the sugar is dissolved and the mixture thickens. At this point add the brandy (if used). When the cake is baked take it from the oven and pour the hot syrup over it.

Serve cold. *Karithopita* will keep for 2 or 3 days.

Greek cooking

Yoghurt Cake

Yaourtopita

700g (1½lb) plain flour
300ml (½ pint) yoghurt
2 teaspoons baking powder
Good pinch salt
225g (8oz) butter

175g (6oz) castor sugar
5 egg yolks
5 egg whites, stiffly beaten
Icing sugar

Cream the butter and sugar until light and fluffy, add the egg yolks one by one, beating vigorously after each addition, then, when this mixture is well blended, add the yoghurt, beating all the while. Sift the flour, baking powder and salt into the creamed mixture and beat again until the flour is thoroughly blended into it. Fold the egg whites into the cake batter and pour it into a greased cake tin, lined with greaseproof paper. Bake at 190°C/375°F/Gas 5 for about 1 hour. Take from the oven and cool on a cake rack (out of the tin). When cool, dust generously with icing sugar.

This is an extremely moist but light cake. Some people like to add grated lemon rind to the ingredients or just a whiff, as it were, of vanilla essence.

Baked Semolina Cake

Halvas Toufournou

450g (1lb) coarse semolina
175g (6oz) butter
225g (8oz) sugar
2 teaspoons baking powder
225–275g (8–10oz) coarsely
  chopped almonds

150ml (¼ pint) brandy
1 tablespoon ground cinnamon
4 egg yolks
4 stiffly beaten egg whites

Syrup

450g (1lb) sugar
900ml (1½ pints) water
1 small piece cinnamon

1 teaspoon lemon juice
150ml (¼ pint) brandy (optional)

Beat the butter and sugar together until very creamy. Add the egg yolks, one by one, beating well after each addition. Add the semolina and, while still beating, the baking powder, cinnamon, brandy and nuts. Finally fold in the egg whites. Pour this mixture into a greased cake tin, lined with greaseproof paper and bake at 190°C/375°F/Gas 5 for 10 minutes, lower the heat and bake until the cake is cooked through, about another 40 minutes. Test with a knife, which should come out clean if the semolina is cooked.

While the cake is baking, make the syrup. Put the sugar, water, cinnamon and lemon juice into a pan, bring to the boil, then cook slowly until the mixture thickens. Remove the cinnamon and stir in the brandy (if used). Pour the syrup (it must be hot) over the cake as soon as you take it from the oven.

For some unknown reason most Greeks call this cake *Halvas Tis Rinas*. Rina is the name of a woman. As one Greek friend of mine explained to me, 'When we talk of *Halvas Tis Rinas* we always know that it is halvas which has been baked in a hot oven, although exactly why I do not know.' The quantity of cinnamon can be reduced to taste.

Greek cooking

Easter Halva Cake

Halvas

450g (1lb) coarse semolina
175g (6oz) butter
175g (6oz) sugar

100g (4oz) chopped blanched almonds
4 eggs
1 teaspoon ground cinnamon

Syrup

450g (1lb) sugar
1.2 litres (2 pints) water

1 teaspoon lemon juice
2.5cm (1in) piece cinnamon

Cream the butter, add the sugar, continue creaming, then add the eggs one by one and beat until the mixture is very creamy indeed. Add the semolina, still beating, and lastly the nuts and the cinnamon.

Half fill a 23cm (9in) round cake tin. Line the tin with greaseproof paper and bake the halva at 190°C/375°F/Gas 5 for about 40 minutes. Boil the syrup ingredients together to a thick syrup and, as soon as you take the halva out of the oven, pour the syrup over it. (Of course, remove the piece of cinnamon.) Cool and cut into squares to serve.

A slightly less elaborate version of the previous recipe.

New Year's Cake

Vasilopita

Vasilopita or New Year's cake is served at the stroke of midnight on New Year's Eve, a date which is one of the most important in the Greek calendar. Celebrating begins fairly early in the evening and relatives and close friends gather together for a party in the largest house in the family circle.

Guests arrive at all times in the evening and are greeted sometimes with spoon sweets (see page 210) and liqueurs or with Turkish coffee and, of course, *kourabiethes* (see page 183) and other Greek delicacies. Groups of boys go from house to house singing the songs of St Basil, the patron saint of the Greek New Year, and come into the house to wish the family good fortune and happiness in the coming year. In return they are offered drinks and *kourabiethes* and usually some hard cash as well.

Good fortune is important and on New Year's Eve the Greeks like to try to discover what their luck is going to be in the coming year. This they try to assess at the gambling table, either at baccara or the roulette wheel. In every house dining tables are stretched to their fullest and overnight Greece becomes one vast Monte Carlo and each house a miniature casino.

Just before midnight all gambling ceases, temporarily, and the table is cleared for the dramatic appearance of the enormous *Vasilopita*, with its lucky coin, another foreteller of luck or otherwise. The arrival of the *Vasilopita* is a moment cherished by all Greeks and even the youngest are allowed to stay up, if they can keep their baby eyes open.

By this time it is midnight, bells clang and shots are fired outside. Everyone begins excitedly to kiss and hug their nearest and dearest and cry happily, 'Hronia polla', which roughly means, 'many happy new years'. All lights are switched on and the host stands ready to cut the cake. He flourishes his knife, then makes the sign of the cross over the cake before he begins to cut the first slice, which is offered either to Panayia (the Holy Mother) or to St Basil. This piece is put aside, then he cuts large slices for the family in order of age, next for the relatives and friends and finally for the servants. What is left over is given the next day to the poor. The traditional *Vasilopita* must be very large. The piece cut for the Holy Mother or St Basil is left on the table and it is expected that during the night it will be collected in person.

The cake distributed, the next moment of excitement is the finding of the

continued

Greek cooking

coin. The fortunate finder is greeted with cheers, for this is a sure sign that he or she will be lucky in the coming year. If the coin is found in the piece left for the Holy Mother or St Basil, this means luck for everyone assembled. If it is in the cake left over for the poor, then to the poor it must go. But until the coin is found there are some tense moments.

After the cake is cut champagne is served and the table cleared once more for gambling, this time in dead earnest, which is continued until the early hours of the morning, often until dawn, which, on New Year's Day, is greeted with a twenty-one-gun salute from Mount Lycabettus. There is, however, still one more chance of good luck, if a handsome blond man should make the first footing across the threshold, then all's right with the world.

New Year's Cake with Yeast

Vasilopita I

1.4kg (3lb) plain flour
50g (2oz) yeast
75g (3oz) sugar
6 eggs
100g (4oz) melted butter

600ml (1 pint) warm milk
1/2 teaspoon salt
1/2 teaspoon sesame seeds
1 teaspoon ground cinnamon

Crumble the yeast into a mixing bowl, add half the milk, the salt, and enough flour to make a batter, about 4 or 5 tablespoons should be sufficient. Cover with a napkin and leave for about 1 hour in a warm place to rise.

Put the remaining flour in another large mixing bowl, make a well in the centre, stir in the yeast batter, add the butter, 5 eggs (one at a time), sesame seeds, and lastly the remaining milk. Mix this thoroughly. Knead for at least 10 minutes. The dough must be stiff, if it is not add more flour; if too stiff, add more milk. Cover the dough again and leave to rise, this time for 3 hours. Put on to a floured board and knead as you would for making a loaf of bread. Tear off a handful and shape the remainder into a cake, before rising this should be 3cm (1 1/2in) thick. Put this into a greased baking tin, lined with greaseproof paper, but leave space for further rising. Take most of the torn-off piece of dough and form it into a long sausage shape with your hands and arrange in a circle on top of the cake. Inside this circle 'write' the number of the coming year with the remaining dough. Cover the dough again with a napkin and let it rise another 2.5cm (1in). Push a silver or golden coin into the cake, beat the remaining egg with a little warm water and sugar and brush this over the top before putting it into the oven. Bake at 190°C/375°F/Gas 5 until brown.

Sometimes chopped almonds are sprinkled over the top of the *Vasilopita* before baking.

This is a typical *Vasilopita* but each family has its own variations of this basic recipe.

Greek cooking

New Year's Cake without Yeast

Vasilopita II

1.4kg (3lb) plain flour
6 eggs
225g (8oz) sugar
125ml (4fl oz) brandy

100g (4oz) melted butter
3 teaspoons baking powder
Juice and grated rind 1 orange
Icing sugar

Separate the egg yolks from the whites. Mix the brandy with the orange juice and rind. Whisk the egg whites until stiff. Beat the egg yolks with the sugar until creamy, add the butter and continue beating for another 5 minutes. Add the brandy and orange then gradually half the flour and half the egg whites. Continue beating until the mixture is thoroughly blended. Add the remainder of the flour and remaining egg whites. Put the mixture into a greased baking tin, lined with greaseproof paper, and bake at 190°C/375°F/Gas 5 for about 1½ hours. Sprinkle with icing sugar and serve cold.

This type of *Vasilopita* is more cake-like than the preceding recipe, which resembles a rich coffee-bread.

Sweet Bread

Koulouria

There are several kinds of *koulouria*. Most popular are the small sesame rings and rolls which the delivery boy brings to the house, yelling as he arrives 'freska koulouria', and with him comes a sweet smell of warm bread and sesame seeds. Or you can buy a *koulouria* at any street corner and munch it on the way to the office or take it with you into the nearest coffee shop and dunk it into your bowl of French coffee. And then there are the sweet *koulouria*, as this recipe, which is more like Danish coffee-bread and also extremely good.

700g (1 1/2lb) plain flour
1 teaspoon baking powder
100–175g (4–6oz) sugar
150g (5oz) butter
2 eggs

Milk or water for mixing
Vanilla flavouring to taste
1 egg white
Pinch salt

Lightly beat the egg white with a little sugar. This is to be used for glazing the *koulouria*. Cream the butter with the remaining sugar until the mixture is very creamy, almost fluffy. Sift the flour with the baking powder and salt into a mixing bowl, add the creamed butter and mix well, preferably with your hands. If the dough is too stiff, add a little milk or water. If too loose, add a little more flour. Break off pieces of the mixture and shape into rolls, buns, or bracelet-size rings. Brush with the egg and sugar glaze and arrange the *koulouria* on a lightly greased baking sheet, lined with greaseproof paper. Bake at 190°C/375°F/Gas 5 for about 15 or 20 minutes, or until the *koulouria* are a golden brown.

There are variations on this theme. For example Cinnamon Rolls are made by using cinnamon instead of vanilla, or you can use sesame, mastic (see page 229) orange or lemon rind, even chocolate.

Greek cooking

Greek Easter Bread

Lambropsomo

900g (2lb) plain flour
50g (2oz) yeast
150ml (1/4 pint) warm milk
600ml (1 pint) lukewarm water
Finely chopped rind 1 orange
Pinch salt

Sesame seeds (see page 228)
5 dyed red eggs (see page 227)
1 egg yolk
1 tablespoon cold water
Olive oil

Dissolve the yeast in the milk, leave for 10 minutes. Gradually add 100g (4oz) of plain flour, cover with a napkin and leave in a warm place to rise overnight.

Next day sift the remaining flour into a large bowl and make a well in the centre. Add salt and half the warm water and gradually work the yeast batter into the centre of the well, adding as you do so the remaining warm water. When all the flour is mixed into the batter, knead the dough for at least 10 minutes. Add the orange peel and if the dough seems to be too loose add a little more flour. Brush a board with olive oil and sprinkle it generously with sesame seeds. Take enough of the dough from the basin and shape into a long loaf, then roll it over and over in the sesame seeds. Pat the loaf until it is about 5cm (2in) high. Take the remaining dough and divide it into 2 pieces rolling them with the hands into long sausage-shape rolls about twice the length of the loaf. Roll one length of dough in the sesame seeds and when well covered place it along one side of the loaf, pressing it down slightly as you work and bring it along one end. Do the same with the other piece but place this on the other side of the loaf. Make 5 depressions in the loaf, one in the centre, the others at the four points of the compass. Into these depressions put the red eggs. Leave covered with a napkin for 3 hours. Beat the egg yolk with the cold water and lightly brush the top of the loaf, bake at 220°C/425°F/Gas 7, for about 45 minutes or until the bread is a golden brown.

There are variations on this theme. The same recipe is used for *Christopsomo*, or Christmas bread, which is decorated with a cross instead of the scarlet eggs and garnished with chopped nuts. The red eggs, according to the Greek Orthodox Church, represent the blood of Christ.

Plaited Bread

Tsourekia

Plaited bread takes the place of the British Hot Cross Bun during the Easter celebrations and is eaten at breakfast on Easter Day.

1.8kg (4lb) plain flour	300ml (1/2 pint) warm milk
175g (6oz) melted butter	Grated rind 1 orange or 1 lemon
100g (4oz) sugar	50g (2oz) yeast
5 beaten eggs	1 teaspoon salt

Dissolve the yeast with 100g (4oz) of flour and the scalded milk and mix to a smooth batter. Cover with a napkin and set aside in a warm place to rise for about 4 hours.

Sift the remaining flour into a mixing bowl, add the salt, sugar, orange or lemon rind, and make a well in the centre. Into this pour the yeast batter, the butter, and 4 eggs (one at a time) working the flour into the centre as you add these ingredients. Work to a fairly stiff dough, sprinkle lightly with flour, then cover with a napkin and leave to rise until it doubles its bulk. Turn on to a lightly floured board and knead, then divide the dough into 3 portions. Roll (with the hands) into long ropes, the ends of which should be thinner than the middle. Plait the 3 pieces and turn the ends under, pressing them down. Arrange on a greased baking sheet, lined with greaseproof paper, and leave to rise once more, about 2 hours. Beat the remaining egg and mix it with 1 teaspoon each of sugar and cold water. Brush this mixture over the top of the bread and bake at 220°C/425°F/Gas 7 for about 20 minutes.

The dough can be made into several plaited buns, or rolled round and round, like a Chelsea bun turned on its side. Mothers of small children often shape the dough into dolls or animals, with a red egg as a face. And quite often coarse sugar is sprinkled over the top and even blanched almonds.

Greek cooking

Honey Pie

Melopita

Pastry

350g (12oz) plain flour
150g (5oz) butter

Pinch salt
1½ teaspoons baking powder

Filling

700g (1½ lb) cottage cheese
175g (6oz) sugar
2 teaspoons ground cinnamon

A 225g (8oz) jar clear honey
5 eggs

First make the pastry. Sift the flour, baking powder and salt together, then rub in the butter. Add enough water to make a stiff dough. Roll out and line a deep 25cm (10in) pie dish.

In a mixing bowl beat the cheese, sugar and half the cinnamon. Add the honey and when this is thoroughly blended, add the eggs, one by one, beating well after each addition. Rub the mixture through a sieve and pour it into the pie dish. Bake at 150°C/300°F/Gas 2 for 45 minutes, then increase the heat and bake for a further 15 minutes. When it is ready insert a knife into the filling, if it comes out clean the pie is ready. Turn off the heat, open the oven door and cool the pie in the oven. Remove and sprinkle with remaining cinnamon. Serve cold.

This is a very good pie and the filling should be thick to get the full flavour.

A recipe not very far removed from those of ancient Greece.

Honey Puffs (with Yoghurt)

Loukoumathes I

The best honey in Greece, according to the Athenians, comes from Hymettos, Athens's nearest mountain, where the bees swarm the mountain slopes sucking the perfumed sweetness from the thyme. However, people living in the region of Delphi also claim that theirs is the best honey, produced on the mountain slopes where the gods used to play. Cooks will, of course, use their own favourite brand of honey.

The puffs which are served with a honey sauce should, according to tradition, 'be as light as thistle-down' and are at their best eaten on a cold winter's night in front of the fire. In Greece, should you have an urge to eat honey puffs but no desire to make them yourself, you go to a *kafenion* or coffee shop where you can order a portion, 6 puffs, with some coffee or perhaps a bottle of Negrita, a mineral water of the Vichy type, which helps to wash down the sweet pastries and puffs so popular throughout the country.

600ml (1 pint) yoghurt
225g (8oz) plain flour
125ml (4fl oz) brandy

Pinch salt
Grated rind 1 orange or lemon
Olive oil for deep frying

Sauce

A 225g (8oz) jar clear honey
Warm water

1 teaspoon lemon juice
1 small piece cinnamon

Beat the yoghurt and the rind together, add the salt and brandy and beat until the mixture is smooth, then gradually add enough flour to make a mixture of dropping consistency. To check whether the mixture is sufficiently pliable, pull some of it from the bowl and if it breaks it is too dry. As it stretches it should have an elastic quality. Leave for 2 hours.

Heat some olive oil in a deep frying pan until it begins to smoke. Drop small spoonfuls of the batter into this, 2 or 3 at a time. The puffs will swell and should be left until they are a golden brown. Take them from the pan and drain on absorbent paper. Cook the syrup ingredients until you have a medium-thick syrup, remove the cinnamon and pour the liquid over the puffs immediately. Serve at once.

continued

Failing yoghurt, sour milk beaten until smooth is excellent as a substitute. The above quantity will make 36 small puffs. Estimate 6 or 8 per person.

Honey Puffs (with Yeast)

Loukoumathes II

450g (1lb) plain flour
50g (2oz) yeast
1/2 teaspoon salt

Lukewarm water or milk
Olive oil

Syrup

A 225g (8oz) jar clear honey
Hot water

1 teaspoon lemon juice
Small piece cinnamon

Dissolve the yeast in a little warm water and mix with 100g (4oz) of the flour. Leave to rise until the batter doubles its size. Add the remaining flour and enough warm water or milk to make a very soft dough. Cover again and let it stand until the dough begins to bubble. This will take 4 or 5 hours.

Heat in a deep frying pan plenty of boiling oil until it begins to smoke. Drop the dough in small spoonfuls into the hot oil 2 or 3 at a time. The puffs will swell and when they are golden brown take them out with a perforated spoon, drain on absorbent paper and serve hot with the honey syrup poured over them.

Syrup. Cook the honey with enough water, cinnamon and lemon juice to make a thickish syrup. Remove the cinnamon before using.

Greek and Balkan experts usually take a handful of the dough and squeeze it through one hand so that a bubble forms on top of the thumb and first finger. Deftly the bubble is knocked off and dropped straight into the pan. For the amateur, and that includes myself, spoons are easier.

Fritters I

Tiyanites

This is really yet another variety of the honey puffs.

450g (1lb) plain flour
2 teaspoons baking powder
125ml (4fl oz) brandy

1/4 teaspoon salt
Juice 1 lemon
Olive oil for deep frying

Syrup

A 225g (8oz) jar clear honey
Ground cinnamon
1 teaspoon lemon juice

Garnish

225g (8oz) ground walnuts

Sift the flour, baking powder and salt into a large bowl. Add enough cold water to make a smooth dough or batter, then add the lemon juice and the brandy.

Heat the oil until boiling, then drop spoonfuls of the batter into it, 2 or 3 at a time. When the fritters are swollen and a golden brown take them from the pan, drain on absorbent paper, and arrange on a platter. Cook the honey with enough warm water, cinnamon and lemon juice to make a syrup and pour this over the fritters. Sprinkle with ground walnuts and serve at once.

Quite often *tiyanites* are served with icing sugar, cinnamon or ground nuts and no sauce.

Greek cooking

Nut Turnovers

Scaltsounia

Filling

225g (8oz) walnuts
225g (8oz) almonds
1 teaspoon ground cloves

1 teaspoon mastic (see page 229)
1 teaspoon ground cinnamon
Honey

Blanch and coarsely grind or crush the walnuts and almonds. Mix with the cinnamon, cloves, mastic and enough honey to blend the mixture without making it too stiff. Leave aside while you make the pastry.

Pastry

225ml (8fl oz) olive oil
225ml (8fl oz) water
1 teaspoon baking powder
Juice 1 lemon

450g (1lb) plain flour
Rose or orange flower water
   (see page 229)
Icing sugar

Mix the first 4 ingredients together, then add enough flour to make a stiff dough. Roll this out to 8mm (1/3in) thick on a floured board. Cut the dough into circles and on each one place a teaspoon of the nut filling (just how much depends on how large you make the circles). Fold the pastry over the filling in the ordinary manner of making turnovers and press the edges of the dough together. Arrange on a greased baking sheet, lined with greaseproof paper, and bake for about 15 minutes at 190°C/375°F/Gas 5 until the pastry is a golden brown. Take the turnovers from the oven, leave until cool enough to handle, then dip them into either orange flower water or rose water and sprinkle with icing sugar.

   Enough for about 25–30 small turnovers.

Sweet Fried Bowknots

Thiples

A favourite Greek tea-time sweet, especially with children.

900g (2lb) plain flour
1 teaspoon baking powder
4 eggs
Pinch salt

Ouzo or orange juice
Water
Olive oil for deep frying

Syrup

350g (12oz) clear honey
300ml (1 1/2 pints) warm water

A little lemon juice
Small piece cinnamon

Garnish

Ground cinnamon
Granulated sugar

Chopped nuts, preferably
   walnuts

Sift the flour and the baking powder, add salt, then the eggs, one at a time, and enough water, flavoured with ouzo or orange juice, to make a stiff dough. If the dough is too loose, add more flour; if too stiff, more liquid. Break off small pieces and roll these out on a floured board until very thin. Cut into strips and tie into bowknots (or any shapes you fancy). Fry in deep, boiling oil until a golden colour. Do not put too many in the pan at the same time. Take the bowknots from the pan with a perforated spoon and place them on absorbent paper until all the *thiples* are finished.

Make a syrup from the honey, warm water and lemon juice. Arrange a layer of the *thiples* on a plate, sprinkle lightly with syrup, cinnamon, sugar and chopped nuts. Arrange another layer and repeat the sprinkling of syrup, cinnamon and nuts. Repeat until all the *thiples* are used up. Most of the syrup pours down into the plate but this can be spooned up and poured over the *thiples* when serving them.

Two other names for *thiples* are *Avgkalamara* and *Xerotiyana*.

Not all Greeks take afternoon tea. It is an adopted custom and rather like the French five o'clock tea.

Greek cooking

Venetian Cakes

Finikia

Finikia is the popular name of honey-dipped cakes called *Melomakarona* and supposed to be taken from a recipe dating back to the Venetians, hence the name.

1.4kg (3lb) plain flour
600ml (1 pint) olive oil
175ml (6fl oz) brandy
Juice 2 oranges
Grated rind 1 orange

1 tablespoon clear honey
1 tablespoon lemon juice
2 teaspoons baking powder
175g (6oz) sugar
1 teaspoon ground cinnamon

Syrup

700g (1 1/2lb) clear honey
1 teaspoon lemon juice

300ml (1/2 pint) water

Garnish

Sesame seeds

Ground cinnamon

Warm the oil and beat it until it becomes almost white. Add brandy, sugar and orange juice and beat for 10 minutes. Work in the flour and continue to work the mixture for 15 minutes, then knead for another 15 minutes. Add the honey, orange rind, baking powder, cinnamon and the lemon juice and knead again for 15 minutes. Shape into very small round cakes. With the back of a fork make designs on the top of the cakes. Arrange on greased baking sheets, lined with greaseproof paper, and bake at 220°C/425°F/Gas 7 for 25 minutes. Leave to cool and meanwhile make the syrup.

Cook the honey and lemon juice with the water to a syrup. Dip the cooled cakes into this and then sprinkle with sesame seeds and cinnamon. This quantity makes a large number of cakes but they will keep for several days, the flavour improving.

Semolina Sweet or Halva

Halvas Simigthalenios

175g (6oz) butter
225g (8oz) coarse semolina

450g (1lb) sugar
600ml (1 pint) water

Garnish

Peeled and chopped almonds

Ground cinnamon

Cook the sugar and water to a syrup. Heat the butter over a low heat to boiling point, using a heavy saucepan. Stir in the semolina and, using a wooden spoon, stir and cook very slowly until the semolina is a light, golden colour. Add the syrup, stir it to blend, then take the pan from the heat, cover with a napkin, and leave on the side of the stove, or turn the semolina into a casserole and bake at 180°C/350°F/Gas 4. Leave for about 15 minutes. By this time the semolina will have absorbed the syrup and be crumbly. Put it into a glass dish, press it down firmly and then turn out to serve. Garnish with almonds and sprinkle with cinnamon.

The secret of halva is the slow cooking until it is a golden brown. Quite often blanched and toasted almonds are added, either chopped or halved.

Greek cooking

Sesame and Honey Sweet

Pastelli

For those who like the flavour of sesame, and I am one, this is a delicious concoction.

450g (1lb) sesame seeds *275g (10oz) clear honey*

Cook the honey and sesame seeds together in a thick-bottomed saucepan very slowly for about 10 minutes, stirring from time to time until the mixture becomes a golden brown. Test it in cold water, if it forms into a ball, then it is ready. Pour it on to a board or a marble slab and pat with the back of a wooden spoon or spatula until it is flat and about 1cm (1/2in) thick.

To store, wrap individually in waxed paper and keep in an airtight box.

This is one of those nice gooey toffee-like sweets that children usually adore.

Apple Compote

Composta Milo

This is simply apples peeled and cut into quarters or halves and put into a saucepan with water, sugar to taste, a small piece of cinnamon stick or cloves and lemon juice, and cooked fairly slowly for about 30 minutes.

Pears, peaches, quinces and other similar fruits are dealt with in the same manner.

Custard

Crema Patisseri

600ml (1 pint) milk
50g (2oz) butter
2 well-beaten eggs

25g (1oz) plain flour or cornflour
Pinch salt

Mix the flour or cornflour to a smooth paste with a quarter of the milk, add the eggs and beat the mixture until it is thoroughly blended. Heat the remaining milk over a low heat, add the flour and egg mixture, stirring all the while to prevent curdling. Continue to cook until the cream thickens and the odour of the raw flour or cornflour has disappeared. Use as a filling for pastries.

Personally I think cornflour is better for this custard than flour. This custard is a good basis for ice-cream but some vanilla flavouring should be added.

Cornflour Pudding I

Crema I

50g (2oz) cornflour
100g (4oz) sugar

900ml (1½ pints) hot milk
Cinnamon

Use a double boiler. Mix the cornflour in a basin with some of the milk to a paste. Bring the remaining milk to the boil in the top of a double boiler and pour it on to the cornflour paste. Stir well and return it to the pan. Add the sugar. Stir and cook until the mixture is very thick. Pour into small glass bowls and sprinkle with ground cinnamon, cool and then chill.

This is the basic recipe for a popular Greek dish which is seldom served after a meal but, like *Rizogalo* (see page 207), eaten between meals as a snack. Sometimes the pudding is sprinkled with ground nuts instead of cinnamon and sometimes a more elaborate version is made, like the following recipe.

Cornflour Pudding II

Crema II

50g (2oz) cornflour
100g (4oz) sugar
3 egg yolks
900ml (1½ pints) milk

Grated rind 1 small orange or
   tangerine
1 teaspoon vanilla essence

Mix the sugar and cornflour with the egg yolks to a paste. Beat until the mixture is smooth. Heat the milk until it is scalding hot, then stir carefully into it the egg and cornflour mixture. Strain (this operation is optional, for if the milk has been added carefully, stirring all the while, the mixture should not have either curdled or become lumpy). Add the orange or tangerine rind and pour the mixture into the top of a double boiler. Cook slowly, stirring all the while until it is thick, then add the vanilla. Pour the crema into glass dishes and sprinkle with cinnamon and coarsely ground nuts. Cool, then chill. It looks and tastes better if you use coarsely ground almonds and pistachio nuts mixed as a garnish.

Rice Pudding

Rizogalo

1.2 litres (2 pints) milk	Ground cinnamon to taste
175g (6oz) sugar	Lemon rind
175g (6oz) pudding rice	2 teaspoons cornflour

Cook the rice with the milk and lemon rind, stirring frequently until the rice is very soft. Add the sugar and the cornflour (mixed to a paste) and continue to cook until the mixture is creamy. Cool and pour into glass dishes, sprinkle with cinnamon, and then put into a refrigerator and leave until ice-cold.

Some Greek cooks like to add 2 well-beaten eggs to the rice. If this is done, the eggs should be beaten into the milk before it is put into the saucepan. However, I think the rice is nice enough without the eggs.

Greek cooking

Wheat and Mixed Fruit

Kolyva

This is a traditional dish, made and eaten by orthodox families forty days after the death of a member of the family and on the anniversary of a death. It has no particular recipe since it is simply wheat boiled until soft and mixed with fruit and pomegranate seeds, all of which have a symbolic meaning. Wheat means everlasting life; fruit, joy and sweetness, and pomegranate seeds, plenty.

The custom of eating *kolyva* dates back to pagan days and was recognized or received the blessing of the Church in the days of Julian the Apostate who, alarmed at the increasing influence of the Christian Church, planned to annihilate the Greek community of Constantinople through the simple expedient of poisoning their Lenten food. This plot, however, was foiled by the timely warning given to them by the Patriarch, Head of the Greek Orthodox Church, to whom the plot was revealed in a dream. He warned his people and told them to eat only wheat during the period of the Lenten fasts. Having been saved from death, the Greeks then dedicated several Saturdays during the year as Soul Sabbaths and to the remembrance of the dead. Then *kolyva* was eaten, it is an improved or revised version of the pagan *pansperima*, a similar dish also eaten in remembrance of the dead.

Chestnut Purée

Kastana Purée

This is prepared in the same manner as the Italian 'Mont Blanc'.

900g (1lb) chestnuts	125ml (4fl oz) brandy
900ml (1½ pints) milk	Salt
75g (3oz) sugar	Whipped cream
1 teaspoon vanilla essence	

Make a slit in the skin of each chestnut and cook in plenty of salted water until the skins will peel off easily, about 15 or 20 minutes. Drain, peel and put into the top of a double boiler with the milk, sugar, a pinch of salt and the vanilla. Cook over hot water until the chestnuts are soft and have absorbed all the liquid. Pour the brandy over the chestnuts, simmer until this is absorbed and then rub them through a coarse sieve. Take small portions and make about 4 discs, roughly 5cm (2in) across. Pile the remaining purée lightly on the top of these discs, it should be light and fluffy, so too much spooning will make it flat. Top with whipped cream and chill before serving. Grated chocolate can be sprinkled over the top of the cream.

Absolutely delicious.

Greek cooking

Preserves and Spoon Sweets
Kompostes ke Ylyka Koutaliou

The offering of 'spoon sweets' to guests is a very old and rather delightful custom. Foreigners, when they first meet it, are apt to be a trifle confused. As one Greek told me, when the tray with its small bowl of preserve, glasses of water, spoons and usually glasses of liqueur is presented to the foreigner, if he does not know the custom, he looks nonplussed. Sometimes he takes the whole bowl of preserve, tries to get through it, then says sadly and with some embarrassment, 'I simply cannot eat it all.'

When the tray thus laden arrives, the guest is supposed to take a spoon, and then a spoonful of the preserve, and eat it. Then he drinks a glass of water, still holding the spoon, which, when he has finished the water, he puts into the empty glass, and returns this to the tray. By this time he is ready to take the glass of liqueur or small cup of Turkish coffee. When he has done all this he should wish his hostess and family happiness and good fortune. If, however, the guest, being a foreigner, is rather shy about doing this, the best thing he can do is to smile brightly and express his thanks.

This offering of spoon sweets is a symbol of Greek hospitality, and also, so my husband was told when he first met the Greek Patriarch in Istanbul, a silent sign that, since everyone eats from the same bowl, it is not poisoned. But this legend dates back ages, further back, even, than the days when we had our royal tasters to prevent poisoning, a well-known custom in days gone by but rarely, of course, known today.

Aubergine Preserve

Melitzanakia Yliko

For this recipe you require ripe but small aubergines. Wash as many as required, score them once with a sharp knife and put into a pan to boil, using not too much water and taking care they do not over cook to a mush. Drain and dry in a napkin. Insert 1 blanched almond deeply into the aubergines, it must be deeply inserted otherwise it will come out during cooking.

Prepare a syrup; mix 450g (1lb) sugar with 50ml (¼ pint) water, with cloves to taste, a small piece of cinnamon and about 1 tablespoon of lemon juice. (Lemon juice prevents the syrup from crystallizing.) When the syrup is almost set, add the aubergines, bring to the boil, then take the pan from the fire. Leave to cool in the syrup, then take out the aubergines with a perforated spoon. Boil the syrup again, let it become thick, return the aubergines, then bring the syrup 2 or 3 times again to the boil. Cool, and pour into sterilized jars or jelly glasses.

A popular recipe in Crete.

Greek cooking

Sour or Morello Cherry Preserve

Vissino Ylyko

1.4kg (3lb) fresh black cherries
2kg (4¹/2lb) sugar

150ml (¹/4 pint) water
Juice 1 lemon

Wash and stone the cherries, but be careful not to break them too much. Put them into a large, shallow pan in layers, sprinkling each layer with sugar. Add the water and cook rapidly until the syrup is as thick as honey, then add the lemon juice, this is to prevent the syrup from crystallizing. Stir gently, skim off any scum which rises to the top. Test the syrup by dropping a little on to a saucer. If the syrup does not spread it is ready.

This type of preserve is a very popular spoon sweet.

Cherry Drink

Vissinada

This is included in this section as the recipe is precisely the same as the previous one, except that more sugar must be added in order to make more syrup.

To make the well-known *vissinada* take from the *vissino* 1 or 2 tablespoons of the syrup and mix this with 150ml (1/4 pint) of iced water or mineral water. It is exceedingly refreshing. The preserve can still be used as a spoon sweet or jam.

Preserve of Bitter Oranges or Lemons

Nerandzaki Ylyko

This is one of the favourite Greek spoon sweets and the unripe oranges or lemons used are dark green and extremely bitter. They are about the size of a table-tennis ball. This is a classical recipe and used by most Greek cooks.

To remove the pips Greek cooks have a small gadget. The main idea is to remove the pips by making a small hole in the fruit and coring it as one does an apple, without destroying the appearance of the fruit.

About 70 or 80 small bitter oranges or lemons	*2kg (4½lb) sugar*

After removing the pips, soak the fruit in cold water for 24 hours. Drain and put into a large pan, add water to cover and bring to the boil, add a teaspoon of soda to keep the skins a bright green. Boil until soft, test with a needle, if the fruit is soft enough it will slip off the needle. It must not be allowed to cook until too soft, otherwise it will become hard during the cooking in the syrup. Drain the fruit and soak it again for several hours in cold water. Drain and dry in a napkin.

Put the sugar into a large pan, add 150ml (1¼ pints) of water, bring to the boil, add the fruit, lower the heat and cook slowly for 5 minutes. Take the pan from the stove, cover, and leave the fruit in the sugar until next day. Take the fruit out with a perforated spoon and place on a large platter. Reboil the syrup and let it become thick. Add the fruit, turn it from time to time and simmer gently until all the dampness of the fruit has been absorbed and the syrup thickly coats the fruit. Cool and seal in jars.

Greek cooking

Preserved Orange Rolls

Nerantzi Yiristo

Another very popular spoon sweet and also a classical Greek recipe. For it you must have large, very thick-skinned oranges which are both ripe and a golden yellow.

First lightly grate as many oranges as you require, about 20, to remove the first bitterness. Wash them well and score deeply through the skin into quarters. Peel these quarters off neatly. Thread a darning needle with strong thread. Roll up the pieces of orange skin tightly as you would a Swiss roll and pass the needle and thread through them, having about 15 or 20 pieces on the thread. Break off the thread and tie the two ends together, you have now a ring or necklace of rolled orange skins. Repeat this until all the orange skin is rolled up and threaded (or 'threddled' as one old countrywoman used to tell me). Fill a large saucepan with water, add the orange skin rolls and cook them until they are very soft. Cool, drain and pour cold water over them. Leave for 24 hours, changing the cold water several times. Drain, remove the threads and dry on a napkin. Prepare a syrup as in the preceding recipe, roughly the same quantity, boil the rolls twice in the syrup, then seal them in jars.

Quince Jelly

Kythoni Peltes

2kg (4 1/2lb) quinces, after
  peeling and cleaning
2.8 litres (5 pints) water
Sugar

3–4 young leaves from the
  ivy-leaf geranium or few
  drops vanilla essence

Wash the quinces, then peel, clean, and stone them, save the skins and stones and put these into a muslin bag and tie it securely. When the quinces have been peeled weigh them to make sure that you have the required weight. When buying the quinces you had better allow for some wastage.

Cut the fruit into thick slices and put these into a large saucepan. Add the water and the muslin bag, cover and cook for 1 1/2 hours. (You cook the skins and stones for their pectin value.) Remove the bag and pour the fruit with its liquid through a jelly bag or a large piece of muslin. Gently squeeze the bag but not too much, otherwise the jelly will become cloudy. (By the way, do not discard the pulp, it is valuable, see following recipe.) Measure the liquid carefully and add 225g (8oz) of sugar for every 450ml (3/4 pint) of juice. Add the geranium leaves, or vanilla essence, and simmer for about 30 minutes. Skim off the foam from time to time. To test for readiness, dip a spoon into the jelly, take it out and let the jelly drip back into the pan. If the last drop sticks to the spoon it is ready. Pour into jars or glasses and next day cover with wax paper and store.

Quince Paste

Pastkithona

A recipe from the island of Cephalonia.

The pulp from preceding recipe
700g (1 1/2lb) clear honey
2.5cm (1in) piece cinnamon
  (optional)

100g (4oz) chopped and blanched
  almonds (lightly fried)
A few halves blanched almonds
A few bay leaves

Rub the pulp through a fine sieve, then mix it with the honey. Put this mixture in a thick-bottomed pan and cook very slowly, stirring from time to time, for about 1 1/2 hours. When the paste comes away from the sides of the pan it is ready. During the last 30 minutes of cooking add the toasted or lightly fried almonds and the cinnamon, this must be removed when the paste is ready. Spread the paste on to a wooden board or better still a piece of marble slab and pat it down, using the back of a wooden spoon or a spatula. It should be about 5cm (2in) thick or just a little less. Garnish with the halves of almonds and leave until cool. Cut into shapes, diamonds, triangles or squares. This kind of paste can be stored in airtight containers. Place in layers, with a bay leaf or two between each layer. Extremely good. The paste should be kept in a cool place.

Quince paste is sold wrapped in cellophane paper in the sweet and pastry shops and the kiosks of Athens and other towns. It is extremely good. I have used the same recipe with guavas with equally good results.

Greek cooking

Quince Cheese

Kythoni Xysto

1.4kg (3lb) quinces
1.4kg (3lb) sugar
300ml (½ pint) water

A few drops vanilla essence
or 1–2 geranium leaves
1 tablespoon lemon juice

Peel the quinces and grate them on a coarse grater. Put them into a large saucepan, add the water and cook gently until the fruit is soft and begins to set. Gradually add the sugar and continue to cook over a high flame until the syrup is thick, at this point add the lemon juice to prevent the syrup from crystallizing. Towards the end add either the vanilla or the geranium leaves, the latter give a more unusual and delicate flavour. Test the jelly by dipping a spoon into it, take up a little of the jelly and drop it back into the pan. When you do this several times and finally the last drop sticks to the spoon like a bubble, then the jelly is ready. Take the pan from the heat, slightly cool and then pour into jars, and seal when cold.

Rose Petal Preserve or Jam

Triandafillo Yliko

You need preferably fresh, large, dark-red rose petals, if possible from the homely cabbage rose.

36 fresh roses, making 2.3 litres
  (4 pints) of rose petals
900g (2lb) castor sugar

1.2 litres (2 pints) water
2 tablespoons lemon juice

Pull off the rose petals and cut off the hard white base which is bitter and also spoils the colour of the jam. Put them into a mixing bowl with a little of the sugar. Gently mix them with your fingers and leave covered overnight. Next day boil the remaining sugar with the water and the lemon juice until the sugar is dissolved and the syrup is rapidly boiling and bubbling. Add the rose petals and continue to cook until the mixture thickens. Pour into hot, sterilized jars and seal.

A favourite breakfast of mine when travelling in the Balkans is brown bread, rather coarse and immensely soft, rose petal jam and fresh butter.

Greek cooking

Cheeses
Tyria

The cheeses of Greece are not spectacular and are made principally for local consumption, although some commercially made Greek cheeses are exported to the vast Greek communities abroad. Most of these cheeses are soft, made either from ewe's milk or goat's milk and traditionally made by shepherds and the peasants. Their quality depends, therefore, entirely on local skill.

The most popular of Greek cheeses is feta, which is a white, soft and crumbly cheese, well salted and equally popular throughout the Balkans. In Greece it has its origin in the mountain regions above Athens. When travel writers talk of their meals with peasants, eating soft, coarse brown bread and white cheese, they mean feta. It is a farmhouse, so-called pickled cheese, but distinct in flavour and, in the right setting, extremely good to eat. It can also be used in cooking, although not in the same manner as a Cheddar or Italian Parmesan cheese.

Feta cheese is made in the same way as all farmhouse cheeses, milk curdled with a starter and rennet, allowed to drain until firm (the whey is kept) and then heavily salted before being packed into wooden kegs. It is left for a month. Feta is not a good traveller, mainly because its water content is too high. It is usually brought into the cities in the large wooden kegs.

One can make a reasonably passable feta at home by curdling milk with rennet and allowing it to drain until the cheese is very firm. When the curd is firm enough to cut into thick slices, it should be generously sprinkled with salt and left for 24 hours, then packed into a wooden keg and left for about 4 days, when it is ready for use.

There is also a slightly more refined feta cheese made from pasteurized milk which is usually exported.

Touloumotyri

A feta cheese packed into goatskins. It has a slightly different flavour and the effect is fascinating when the skin is opened, exposing its pure white inside.

Telemes

Another feta-type cheese made into squares, and rather more heavily salted. It ripens more quickly than feta but the two are often confused.

Kopanisti

This is a 'blue' feta cheese which has been allowed to coagulate longer and is, therefore, of a finer texture. It is also allowed by certain processes to gather a blue mould which, in time, is kneaded into the cheese. It has a sharp, rather peppery flavour and is recommended to those who like to try different cheeses.

Myzithra

A soft, cottage cheese made from the whey which is drained from the feta and mixed with fresh milk. The Greeks find many more uses for cottage cheese than we normally do in Britain and one of their specialities is the cottage cheese pie (see page 226) which I highly recommend.

Greek cooking

Kefalotyri

A hard cheese, very salty with a hard rind, used as a Parmesan. It is made in various parts of the country and known under several names. It is used mainly as a cooking cheese and can be easily grated. Its name comes from its shape, which is like a hat, or *kefalo*.

Pinthos

A better class *kefalotyri*.

Kasseri

A firm, white cheese, mildly flavoured but somewhat softer and much used in cooking as a grating cheese. Also eaten fresh.

Gruyère

The Greek version of the famous Swiss cheese. It is made from ewe's milk and, when it is good, it is very good. When not, is just a poor imitation.

Agrafa

An improved version of the Greek Gruyère and usually of high quality.

Anthotyro

A goat's cheese from Crete, eaten at all times of the day. Firm, with not too strong a flavour, it is extremely popular with Cretans, who like it served with grapes.

Antholyti

This is a round, pale-yellow cheese which comes in two or three sizes. It has a mottled, thick rind as wrinkled as a relief map.

Anari

Goat or ewe's milk cheese which, when kept, looks like a ripe Gorgonzola. It can be bought in salted squares or round like a pudding. Greek-Cypriot.

Halorini

A cheese made usually from ewe's milk folded over like dough and filled with pounded coriander. Greek-Cypriot.

Manouri

A sweet, soft cheese when it is fresh but hardens as it ages.

Gravieri

A similar cheese to Gruyère and made in Crete. Like the Greek Gruyère it can be extraordinarily good.

Parnossus

Another of the white cheeses made from ewe's milk.

Sundries and Coffee
Thiafora Kafes Mavros

Actually Greek coffee is Turkish coffee. Coffee is said to have been introduced into Europe, via Turkey, during the reign of Suleyman the Magnificent (1520–66) by a merchant of Aleppo who returned to his home city richer by 50,000 ducats. The Arabic name was, and still is, *kahveh*, signifying the queller of appetites. At first it excited the suspicions of the more puritanical Moslems and the new coffee houses, which were opening up throughout the Ottoman Empire, were viewed with apprehension. But Suleyman was as wise as he was magnificent and allowed them to continue.

Since then coffee drinking in special coffee houses has been a habit of the Balkan peoples. Sitting for hours in a coffee house staring into space and sipping a small cup of coffee is a recognized way of living. The waiter brings the customer glass after glass of water, sometimes yet another cup of coffee, and the classical coffee drinker sits and stares, or talks politics, or, if he is old-fashioned, gurgles leisurely through his *nargileh* or hubble-bubble. If you want to see something typical of the Balkans while in Athens, simply wander along to the coffee shops, *kafenion*, in and around Ommonia; there sit men up from the country, each in his favourite coffee house with his cronies.

However, if you prefer it, you can order French coffee in Athens and in other larger cities and this means coffee with milk. Athens has many coffee bars, they grow up overnight. I was there when the first Sputnik completed its successful orbit around the earth; overnight Athens had its 'Sputnik' coffee house.

When ordering Turkish coffee you need guidance. You must know whether you want it with sugar, a little sugar, or no sugar at all. And then you must know whether you want it well-boiled or not. Most people who are unused to Turkish coffee prefer it medium-boiled and medium-sweet, and for this one asks for *metrio vrasto*. Those who like their coffee very sweet should ask for *vary ylyko*, strong and sweet. But those who, like myself, prefer all coffee, even Turkish, without sugar must ask firmly for *sketto vastro*.

For each cup of coffee (small *mokka* cups) you require 1 cup of water, 1 heaped teaspoon of coffee powder, finely ground and sugar to taste. It is usual not to make more than three or, at the most, 4 cups of coffee at a time. Put 3 coffee cups of water into the pot and bring this to the boil. Add the coffee and let it rest on the top of the water, then add sugar to taste. Bring the water once more to the boil, take it from the heat, let the froth which has risen die down and then return the pot to the fire again. Let the water boil and froth again, take it from the fire and when the froth has died down repeat the process. But this time stir the coffee well into the water as it boils, at the same time trying not to lose too much of the froth. Pour the coffee at once into the coffee cups, evenly distributing the froth, for this brings luck. The more froth you have the more luck.

Among the Greeks in Istanbul there are those who can read the future in the coffee grounds left in the cup after drinking, but I found less of this in Greece. Which is sad, for such fine futures are foretold from the thick mass of coffee grains left in the cup after being turned upside down and allowed to cool.

Salepi

This is a drink sold in the early hours of the morning or very late at night. It is a hot, sweet infusion of orchid tubers, rather like milk in appearance, but to my taste quite insipid. The vendor carries his equipment in a brass container which includes a charcoal stove to keep the salepi hot. It was once a popular British drink, but is today quite unknown.

Tisanes

In most parts of Greece as well as in the islands the people use all the herbs of the fields as well as those of the gardens. Each herb has its own special quality and flavour and many are turned into a tisane, or tea, for curing this or that complaint. Many Greek housewives have herbal recipes for all domestic ailments.

Punch or Wine Cup

Bowle

1 bottle champagne
2 bottles dry white wine
150ml (1/4 pint) brandy
2 bottles sparkling mineral water

1 sliced orange
1 sliced banana
1 small tin cubed pineapple

Mix the champagne, brandy and wine, add the fruit, together with the pineapple juice. Put the bowl in which you have mixed the ingredients on a bed of crushed ice. Add the water just before serving. If a sweeter wine cup is required, add about 225ml (8fl oz) of syrup, but this would make a very sweet punch even sweeter.

Instead of champagne a sparkling wine can be used.

Yoghurt

Yaourti

Yoghurt belongs to the species buttermilk, sour milk and cottage cheese and is made by adding a bacterial culture or bacillus to fresh milk, in Greece this means, usually, sheep's milk. There are several stories concerning its origin. One is that the Turks discovered it when they were wandering nomads and carried their milk in gourds slung over the backs of camels. The sunshine and the constant jolting turned it thick and sour, and made the first yoghurt. Another story is that the early inhabitants of Greece used to leave their goat and sheep milk exposed to the bacteria of the open air and it developed a new character which they liked. So yoghurt became a staple part of the people's diet.

Many things are claimed for yoghurt; it is a cure for stomach troubles of a minor kind; it helps dyspeptics and those afflicted with dysentery. A large bowl of yoghurt taken after an evening's heavy drinking will, it is claimed, avert a hang-over, while others claim that if you already have a hang-over a bowl of yoghurt will go a long way towards sending it away. Many of the really old people living in the mountains of the Balkans claim that yoghurt is the secret of long life.

In cooking it has many virtues; food can be marinated in yoghurt, it blends with almost all vegetable dishes and can be used in gravies, in cakes and scone making, in fact, its virtues are almost endless.

Yoghurt can be made at home quite simply. All that is required is a teaspoon or so of the commercially prepared yoghurt mixed with milk.

Recipe. Bring 1.2 litres (2 pints) of milk to the boil, pour it into small earthenware dishes or cups and leave until it is blood hot. Dilute 2 teaspoons of commercially made yoghurt with some cold milk and pour a little of this into each dish or cup, disturbing the milk as little as possible. Cover with a flannel cloth to keep warm, or put into a warm oven, without the heat turned on. Leave until the yoghurt is very thick. Serve cold.

Greek cooking

Cheese Pie

Tyropita

450g (1 lb) feta cheese
  (see pages 218–219)
450g (1 lb) cottage cheese
Chopped fresh parsley to taste
Nutmeg to taste
About 75–100g (3–4oz) melted butter

20 sheets filo pastry
  (see pages 177–8)
50g (2oz) sifted plain flour
125ml (4fl oz) cream
4 eggs

Test the feta cheese. If it is too salty soak it in water for a while, drain and put it in a mixing bowl. Add the cottage cheese and blend. Break in the eggs, one by one, beating each well into the cheese. Mix the flour with the cream, then stir this into the cheese mixture. Line a large, shallow baking-tin with butter and lay in it 10 sheets of filo pastry, each sheet brushed with melted butter. Spread the cheese mixture on the top sheet, then cover with the remaining filo, spreading each one lightly with butter. Turn in the edges of the pastry to keep the filling from oozing out and sprinkle the top sheet lightly with water to prevent this from curling upwards. Score the top through the first 3 or 4 layers of pastry into serving size pieces, diamond or oval shapes. Bake at 190°C/375°F/Gas 5 for about 45 minutes. Cool a little before serving. Serve warm for Greek taste; hot for British.

This is a popular Lenten dish and also eaten during *tyrini*, or cheese week, the last week of the pre-Lenten carnival, locally called *apokries*. The word *apokreo* literally means fast from meat and applies to the many days of fasting which the Greek Orthodox Church ordains. In its plural form *apokries* has today come to mean two weeks of meat fasting, called *kreatines*, and one of cheese eating called *tyrini*. These three weeks constitute the Greek Carnival, much entertaining, masked balls, streamers, noise, and confetti, in fact, all the fun of Carnival and certainly a time to visit Greece.

Tyropita can also be made with all cottage cheese instead of half cottage and half feta cheese.

Rice Omelette

Omeletta Me Rizi

5 eggs
3 tomatoes
6 tablespoons boiled, salted
   long-grain rice

Butter
Salt and pepper
Breadcrumbs and flour
Sugar

The tomatoes should be large and firm. Peel, and slice them thickly and sprinkle them with salt, pepper and sugar. Mix enough fine breadcrumbs with flour to make a coating for the tomatoes. Dip each slice of tomato into this and fry them on both sides in hot butter. Put aside and keep hot.

Beat the eggs, add salt and pepper and then the rice. Spread this out in a frying pan and cook slowly until the egg is set. When it is cooked put the omelette on a dish and garnish it with the fried tomatoes.

Sometimes finely chopped, fried onions are added to the rice and eggs before cooking. A most substantial kind of omelette.

Scarlet Easter Eggs

Kokkina Avga

There are many ways to colour eggs. They can be painted or dyed in a harmless powder dye, or you can simply cook the eggs until hard in water which has been treated with cochineal or other red cooking colouring.

Greek cooking

Aniseed

Anise

The seeds of a small aromatic plant and a member of the parsley family. As children we first meet the flavour in liquorice sweets. It is greatly used in Oriental and Balkan cooking and is popular as a pickling spice.

In ancient Greece a sprig of anise was hung over the bed to prevent bad dreams and nowadays herbalists prescribe a teaspoon of anise seeds in a glass of hot milk sweetened with honey as a cure for insomnia. Anise is also made into a tisane and served as a cold tea in hot weather.

Cumin

Cumin

An aromatic fruit, so small it is usually referred to as a herb. It has a slightly bitter flavour and when it is not available it can be substituted by the caraway seed. Cumin flavours much of the Oriental cooking and is highly prized as an appetite stimulant. Jesus spoke of it when he was exhorting the Scribes and the Pharisees . . . 'ye pay tithe of mint and anise and cumin and have omitted the weightier matter of the law, judgment, mercy and faith.'

Sesame Seeds

The product of a small annual plant grown extensively in various parts of the Balkans, Russia and the East. The seeds are small, honey-coloured (sometimes called white) and are used in Greece in flavouring breads, rolls, biscuits and cakes.

It is also a main flavouring in the commercially made halva. Gives a rich toasted flavour to breads, etc.

Mastic

Mastiha

Small, clear crystals coming from an evergreen, resinous shrub. It is used a great deal in Balkan cooking. Mastic is one of the important Greek exports and in the days of the Turkish occupation the ladies of the Sultan's harem were allowed as pocket money the proceeds from the mastic gum sales. In those days the sales were considerable and the main growing area was the island of Chios, which became important as a money earning island through its mastic, so was granted its own parliament. The flavour is faintly like liquorice, a word of Greek descent, which means sweet root.

Mastic gum is produced by making incisions in the bark of the main trunk and branches to make the shrub 'cry'. On the ground around the shrub is sprinkled a layer of fine sand on to which the 'tears' of the tree drop. These tears are the crystals and the work of sorting them out for size, colour and quality is still done by hand.

Rosewater

The best rosewater came formerly from Bulgaria from the famed rose gardens. It is an important ingredient in Balkan and Oriental cooking and used to be so in British cooking. Imparts a fragrant perfume and flavour when used with discretion.

Orange Flower Water

Nerole or neroli is an essential oil distilled from orange blossoms and used in flavouring confectionery. Orange flower water is the fragrant liquid collected from the distillation of the oil.

Greek cooking

Wines
Krassi

Wheat, olive oil and wine compose the holy trinity of the Greek diet. Of these only olive oil is obtained without sweat and labour. The goddess Athene was generous in her gift of the olive tree to the people of Greece as it requires so little attention. But wheat and wine, these mean hard work and so, perhaps, it is logical that both Demeter, the Goddess of Grain, and Dionysus, the God of Wine, in the old pagan days should have been closely associated with the religious rites and ceremonies of the people.

Bread and wine form the components of the greatest mystery in the Christian Church and, therefore, it is fitting that the harvesting of wheat and grapes should be the two main harvests of the year, taking precedence over the profitable olive harvest.

Bread and cheese with a bunch of grapes (or a glass of wine) is the usual meal for many Greek peasants and, according to doctors, this is a full diet, the grapes alone are enough. In days gone by the rules of health and hygiene were closely allied to the teachings of the Church and its religious rituals. For example, the first eating of the grape in Greece is on the day of Our Lord's Transfiguration, 6 August. On this day the grape-growers bring a basket of their choicest fruit to the priest, who blesses it with the words: 'O Lord, bless this season's fruit of the vine so that it may bring health and joy.'

Wines
Krassi

In still more ancient times, the god, Dionysus, was worshipped and the grape harvest *(tyrgitis)* was a time for the gathering together of the agricultural workers, and began with an incantation to the god, Dionysus.

Greeks have drunk wine since the beginning of time. Their present habit of dipping bread into wine and olive oil, even in the early morning, is a survival of an ancient custom. Wine is a part of the Greek heritage. To quote Hesiod: 'After the toil of the day is over, should your desire be to eat your food in peace and drink a glass of wine to settle yourselves, it is a worthy ambition.'

The Greeks believe they have the finest grapes in the world and, say they logically, the best wine. In earlier days Greek wines were sent throughout the known world, even as far as India. Unhappily the Indians long ago lost their taste for wines. Greek wines vary enormously, principally because the grape growers do not confine themselves to a particular brand of grape, of which there are at least five hundred different varieties. This means that the wine producers must make their wine from the grapes as they come in. One vineyard alone will send six or more different kinds, so that it is impossible for the wine producers to conform to a uniform quality. The only possible exception to this is the wine produced in the Mesogeia, that is, the interior of Greece as opposed to the coastal areas. Here there are quite large tracts of land under cultivation producing one variety of grape, the Savvatiano. This grape in turn produces a retsina wine of a fairly uniform quality, said to be the best in the country.

To show the diversity of Greek wines, at the 1958 Daphni Wine Festival fifty different kinds of wine were offered for exhibition. However, the ancient Greeks could doubtless have produced as many or even more. Then, as now, there were white, red and rose wines, dry and sweet, and light and heavy. This wide choice of wines adds pleasure to the tourists' eating and drinking. But such is the diversity that when one finds a wine especially to one's liking and notes with care the name and the year of its vintage, another bottle of the same type might be a sorry disappointment. Equally, a bottle of wine which may seem displeasing can have a sister bottle which is quite good.

Probably the most controversial wines of Greece are the retsinas, which, although the national drink of the Greeks, are wines which many people, including Greeks, find overpowering. A retsina is a wine (either white or red, but usually white) which has been deliberately and heavily resinated. To those who acquire a taste for it, it can be a wine of pleasant distinction.

continued

Greek cooking

The origin of retsina wine is interesting. In the days before casks and bottles the Greeks kept their wines in goatskins and then poured pitch-pine on top in order to caulk or preserve them. The Greeks, therefore, expected their wines to taste of resin or pitch-pine and continued to add this flavouring after both casks and bottles had been invented. Many critics say that adding resin to wine is spoiling it. I do not agree. Drinking retsina wine on a sea shore beneath the pines, or in the pine woods themselves, is a pleasure which remains long in the memory. The fragrant scent of the pine needles mingles with the taste of the wine and enhances the flavour of what one is eating.

Retsina wines belong to the tavernas of the cities and countryside, and it is on the quality of the retsina that the reputation of a taverna is made or lost. The new wines arrive in the tavernas in the middle of September, when waiters can be seen busily scrubbing out their barrels to receive them. On 26 October, St Demetrius's Day, these new wines are served and thousands of barrels of retsina are tapped. Regular taverna goers are invited to attend the first tasting of the new season's retsina. This first evening is an anxious one for the proprietors for, on this first tasting, depends the custom of the following year. If the retsina is good the word flies swiftly throughout the district; if bad or indifferent, then with equal swiftness everyone is told. And at the end of a convivial evening the patrons may sing:

Retsina wine,
With you I'll die,
No earthly joy,
With you can vie.

To visit one or other of the private wine presses is for most people a definite holiday attraction. Just outside Athens, at Markopoulo, there are several private presses and it is here that some of the best retsina is produced. At the time of the grape harvest the roads in the area are cluttered with a constant stream of traffic of all kinds, horse-drawn carts, donkeys and donkey carts, mules and lorries, all loaded with grapes, all making their contribution to the flow of grapes destined for the commercial wine presses or the smaller, private ones.

Those grapes which come to the private presses are unloaded through an opening in the wall and tumbled on to the cement floor of the pressing room. Here several men will be waiting ready, with feet bare and trousers rolled up to the thighs, to stamp the grapes. Some, with the aplomb with which a Spanish dancer wears a rose, will fasten a bunch of grapes over their ear and, as they begin to work with precision and skill, they sing songs of the grape, their voices getting louder as the tempo of the stamping rises. As the grapes are loosened from their skins the precious liquid flows through an opening into a vat below and the mass becomes denser and denser until only the stems and skins remain. As each batch of grapes is finished, the skins are swept away and another supply of grapes is attacked. The juice is then tested for its sugar content and pumped away into the tank-like lorries which are standing by. Over the district the faint but pleasant smell of must hangs for days.

For those who might like to indulge in a little amateur grape trampling there is a taverna at Liopessi which has its own press and has become popular with patrons on this account. Carved on the barrels here are many famous names of those who have allowed themselves a little fun.

But not all the wines of Greece are resinated. Far from it. In the average restaurant the wine list will contain at least twenty or more different names and, if you want advice, the best people to ask are the taverna or restaurant owners or waiters. They will be refreshingly frank on the subject. Most Greek wines are extremely cheap so that it does not cost much to buy experience. The resinated wines are usually golden, although there are red and rose retsinas. Most Greek wines of any character are white, with the main exception of the well-known Nemean.

There are one or two wine-drinking tavernas in Athens where you can sit and nibble at *mezethakia* and try wines from the cask for as long as you like. It makes a delightful holiday occupation for the tourist.

The following list of Greek wines is by no means comprehensive. It is meant merely as a guide to the more popular wines, a starter for the wine drinker who should, after his first local initiation, go adventuring into this field of research alone.

Retsina

This comes from many parts of the country and is of three types but many varieties. Generally retsina is a golden wine but there is *kokkinelli* which is rose colour, and *kokkino* which is red. Towards the end of an evening of eating and drinking, many Greeks like to take a glass of retsina wine mixed with soda or mineral water. It is not unlike a light champagne in taste and is said to help against having a hangover.

Greek cooking

Mantinea

A light wine of the Riesling type and popular with most foreigners. It comes from the Peloponnese which produces what the French call *petits vins*. From the same area is a type of Hock called Tour La Reine.

Domestica

Both red and white and considered as a reasonably priced good table wine.

Hymettus

A very inexpensive wine of the Pouilly type.

Kamba

A rather dry white wine.

Zitsa

Very pleasant sparkling wine, somewhat grandly called a champagne.

Nemean

A rich, red wine known locally as 'Lion's Blood' because of its alcoholic strength. Comes from the Peloponnese.

Mavrodaphne or Maurodaphne

An exceedingly sweet, heavy wine for serving with fruit or dessert. It is also used as a main ingredient in a wine cup or bowl.

Castel Danielis

A red wine of the Burgundy type, belonging to the slightly higher priced groups.

Naoussis Boutari

An almost black wine, very powerful and considered by many to compare with the Medoc wines. Very dry, 'as dry as a wood-file,' I was told as I tried it. And how right this was: it almost rasped my tongue.

Broussiko

A sweet, port-wine type from the Cyclades.

Romola

A rosé wine of the Anjou type, coming from the islands of Zante and Cephalonia.

Chateau Decilie

A wine which has the distinction of being made from grapes grown in the royal vineyards.

Chevalier di Rhodi

A medium-priced red wine from the Island of Rhodes.

Samos wines

Samos has long been famous for its rich and golden wines, somewhat sweet and very strong. Those who care to follow the excellent advice of Lord Byron and 'Fill high the bowl with Samian wine', might also emulate the islanders and add some water to it. Greeks have added water to their wines for centuries. We read in the *Iliad* that when Aias and Odysseus called on Achilles in his tent at Troy, the latter, wishing to show real hospitality, called to his attendants, 'Let there be stronger wine, wine without water.' There is also a widespread superstition that water must be added to wine during those months without an 'r' in them. Probably a wise precaution against too much alcohol during the trying hot months.

Santorini

The wines of this volcanic island are favoured by the Vatican for its communion wines. They have a strong, brackish flavour which comes from the minerals in the ground. These same minerals also add to the potency of the Santorini wines and most islanders insist that their glasses must be diluted by one-fourth of water. But, even so, the islanders, with a sly smile, insist too much of their wine turns a man crazy, a fact which appears to concern them not at all.

Greek cooking

Rhodes

An island strongly influenced by the Italians, who occupied it for a long time. Most of its wine is even cheaper than that on the mainland and follows an Italian pattern, more especially the liqueurs and aperitifs.

Crete

King Minos is probably the best of the Crete wines, or at least the best known. It is a pleasant, golden wine best served ice-cold. Kritica, a dark, red wine, rather dry, like the Naoussis, also comes from Crete.

Commanderia

A heavy Madeira-type wine from Cyprus, one of the best-known Cypriot wines.

Brandies and Cognacs

There are several Greek brandies, some of which are very good. Probably the best-known brands are Varvaressou and Metaxas.

Ouzo

A clear spirit, distilled from the grapes, usually the by-product of the wine making. It can be taken neat or with water as a chaser. Most foreigners find it more palatable to mix ouzo with water and add a cube of ice. This sends it cloudy and white. The Turks, by the way, call ouzo 'Lion's milk'. It has a strong aniseed flavour and is not only the drink of the Greeks but of the neighbouring countries. It is taken as an aperitif and has the advantage that it does not paralyse the palate for anything to follow. In hot weather it is one of the very best of drinks. Ouzo drinkers insist that one should always eat when drinking.

An evening's over-indulgence in ouzo (or *arak* or *raki*), British troops claimed, produced the morning after, a blackout after drinking a glass of water: as though this were an economic drink for a drunk. I have not myself experienced this and my husband, who has consumed ouzo in large quantities in his time, says this story is pure fantasy.

Ouzo is both privately and commercially made and varies in quality. The best is distilled from grapes and filtered several times. In some parts of the Arab world, in Iraq for instance, ouzo is distilled from dates and has quite another taste. Village-made ouzo is really fiery stuff, rough, and to be treated with real respect. You do not add water when drinking ouzo with a Greek peasant, he would think this incredibly cissy.

Mura

This is a somewhat startling drink, a pure white liquid which the drinker is supposed to toss off in the nonchalant manner of the vodka drinker.

Mastiha

This is sometimes described as 'a liqueur flavoured with gum mastic'. Mastic is a low branching tree with shiny leaves and belongs to the pistachio family. It grows in several parts of the world, but mostly in Chios, which has over four million trees. I have not been able to like this drink but there are many who do, including foreigners.

Beer

Greek beer is very palatable and based on German beer. Like many things in Greece, this is a monopoly of the firm Fix, which is a corruption of the German name Fuchs. Herr Fuchs was a Muenchener who followed one of the Bavarian princes chosen for the Greek throne. He began to make beer and the family, now Hellenized, have been making beer for several generations.

Greek cooking

Greek cooking

Greek cooking

Greek cooking